MAMA JANE'S PEARL

A BIOGRAPHY OF VERA WALLACE

GREGORY MCEWAN

REVILO
PRESS

MAMA JANE'S PEARL: A BIOGRAPHY OF VERA WALLACE

In loving memory of Vera Petrona Wallace,
Mama Jane's Pearl, the song in our hearts.
Mother, 'Granny', Great-grandmother,
You are missed.

Also
In loving memory of Wayne Fitzgerald McEwan
A.K.A (Sticky)
1964-2020

A Note on Language

Throughout this book, you will find Jamaican words, phrases, and expressions that reflect the voice and rhythm of the people and places that shaped Vera Wallace's life. A full glossary with pronunciation is included at the end of the book for reference.

1

AUNT P

I can hardly remember the last time I took steps on my own, for I am an old, crippled woman. It is nearly Christmas; 1922 is quickly coming to a close. I am Sarah Pickersgill-Hoffstead, but around these parts, they call me Aunt P. I'm almost sixty years old—not so old—but I tell you, with these useless limbs, I feel ancient. Oh bwoy, di tings we tek fi granted.

I remember the days of my youth—I was agile as a cat. I could scale any fence before you could say, *"cat lick mi tail."* I smile wide now, for that's just an old Jamaican saying. All Jamaicans know it—if you can do something before a cat turns to lick its tail, it means you're fast. And bwoy, was I ever quick. Back then, everyone in the district of Clark's Town knew how swift Sarah Pickersgill was. But that was long before I lost the use of my legs. Now I'm dependent on my children to care for me. But I was the one who spent many nights nursing them, changing their nappies.

It's early in the morning, and I like to savour the Jamaica sunrise. So Albert, my good son, lifted and carried me out to the veranda of my old wooden house just before dawn. A good boy, my son is. God knew what he was doing when he gave me a son. The good Lord moves in mysterious ways, for when I found my husband Henry, the thought had never crossed my mind that he could ever die.

My Henry was a good man. He gave me three strong children—two girls and a boy. And though the eldest felt she was too good for Clark's Town and went off to America, the other two stayed with their mama. God bless my Albert and my daughter Esme.

I've always called this strong board house my home. In fact, I was born in this very place, back when there was only one room. I shake my head now as I gaze at my hands in my lap, memories of youth swarming my mind. I can't help but smile. God has been good to me—for after He took my folks home, He didn't leave me alone. He sent me a man. A good man, too.

It's time to close my eyes for a few moments and let the sounds and smells of my surroundings bring me peace. The sun is up now. I can feel it on my face. I hear the echo of the axe as it chops into chunks of logwood in the backyard. I'm smiling again.

"Mi bwoy Albert... God bless him..."

The crowing of several roosters echoes in the distance, one after the other, like they're luring each other into a crowing contest. Far off, I hear the beak of a woodpecker against a tree trunk. It won't be long before my breakfast is served—I can already smell Esme's homemade coconut oil. The aroma of onions and scotch bonnet peppers has just crept up my nostrils...

"Mawnin, Aunt P."

My eyes open quickly. I see my neighbour standing at the gate.

"Yuh deh tek early mawning sun, Aunt P."

Mary Jane Hall stands with her hands akimbo, her green eyes smiling at me behind her silver-rimmed spectacles.

"Yes, Ma Jane. How yuh do?"

She shifts her broad-rimmed hat atop her head of cascading brown curls.

"Nuh too bad, mi sis. Cyan complain."

Mary Jane skillfully holds her pipe between her lips as she speaks, exhaling smoke from both mouth and nostrils with every word. Everyone in Clark's Town—if not all of Trelawny—knows Mary Jane

Hall. Or Mama Jane. The woman is a healer; she tended to my Henry's ailments more than once.

She finally removes the pipe, takes a deep breath, and coughs. She taps it, extinguishing the fire with her thumb.

"Gal, mi chest give mi a warm time."

She slaps her chest with her palm.

"A suh it guh," I reply.

I look into Mary Jane Hall's green eyes and see nothing but strength. She can't be much older than I am—maybe just over fifty or so. She's a matriarch to the entire district. I remember taking my own children to her house just for her to give them a good flogging. Mary Jane Hall can't abide unruly children, especially her own.

As for her household—the brown-skinned woman known as Mama Jane, Miss Mary, Ma Jane, even Miss Hall—isn't one to trifle with. As God-fearing as she is, Mary Jane Hall will curse and tell you bad words. And she'll never take them back once she's done. She speaks the truth, whether or not you like it.

Her green eyes are fixed on my hands now—by God, the damned arthritis betrays me again.

She grins and shakes her head.

"Nuh mind, gyal. Mi a-guh send yuh sumting fi di pain. Tata Joe wi bring it cum."

Mary Jane's word is her bond. I needn't ask when her husband will bring it. I know it will come.

Without another word, Mary Jane taps the ashes from her bone pipe into the palm of her hand—and eats it. In all my years, I've never seen a man do that. But a great woman does. And though I can't understand the reason, I don't question her.

I raise my hand to shield my eyes from the Wednesday morning sun and watch Mary Jane Hall walk briskly down the lane toward her house. The hem of her long skirt drags through patches of grass, and her wavy brown hair, streaked with gray, cascades over her shoulder.

Mary Jane Hall has her hands full, I'm sure of it. Her husband, Joseph Williams—or Tata Joe, as we all call him—is a good man. Almost as good as my Henry was. But my Henry was different from any other man. The good Lord broke the mold when He made him. My Henry was always in charge—a real man ah yaad.

But in Mary Jane's house, the whole district knows who's boss. And it sure isn't Tata Joe.

I didn't spend much time in school, but at least I learned to read a little. I remember one of the first things they taught us at Clark's Town Primary was the geography of our land. Fourteen parishes in Jamaica. I was born right here in Trelawny, Clark's Town. I live in Top Town, on the east side of the main road. On the west side is Bottom Town.

Reader, you must be wondering why this old woman is babbling about everything and nothing at the same time. And I'm sure you think what you're about to read is all about me.

You're wrong.

My part in this is brief. Before this story ends, I will be long gone. But I have my own role to play, short as it is. And if you keep reading, you'll find out what that is.

I'm only here to open the door and welcome you in. And I'm doing it at the right time. As my dear grandmother always said, "nuttin happen before di time cum."

I'm looking down the lane now, watching Mary Jane Hall step into her little house. So now you know why I'm here.

I'm opening the door into the lives of a household of women—the home of Mary Jane Hall and her girls. But it's the life of her youngest grandchild you'll learn about.

And I can't even tell you her name, for she's not yet born. How do I know it's a girl? We women just know—by looking at the belly.

I throw my head back and laugh now, knowing full well you think I'm mad as hell. But don't fret, reader. It won't be long. She's on her way.

And don't you think for a moment that Aunt P is crazy.

As I said before—I'm only here to open the door... and do my little bit.

———————

———————

I ENJOYED A LOVELY BREAKFAST RIGHT HERE ON MY VERANDA, AND NOW, with mi belly full, I sit looking out in the distance. It is a hot December day—so hot, I doubt I'll be able to stay out in the sun much longer. Well, at least the old orange tree offers some shade.

Albert and Esme, my good children, have taken care of everything, so I need only rest this old tired body and finish my little bit. Did you think I'd forgotten? A few days have passed since I spoke with Mary Jane Hall by my front gate. It is Sunday now, the day before Christmas, and as I tap my fingers against the arm of my old wooden chair and hum along with the Christmas songs on the radio, I watch the children play.

Most are from Top Town, but I can see a few that don't belong—little friends who've crossed over from Bottom Town, just by Mr. Chin's bakery.

I sent my daughter, Esme, over to see Mary Jane Hall this morning. The woman has been busy for days, looking after those three little girls. You see, Tata Joe has no children of his own, for when he met Mary Jane, she already had one daughter. I don't know if she has any other children, but I know Bernice—and I've heard of her father, John Bolt from Minard Hill in Brown's Town.

Bernice is with child again, due any day now. She already has two little girls—Virginia, or Virgie, who's nearly five, and little Lela, just two. Like I told you before, Miss Mary Jane Hall is the matriarch. Bernice might've brought those girls into the world, but Miss Hall does the rearing. She's even taken in her little niece, Lucile Simpson, after her sister Amanda died.

Reader, I tell you, Miss Mary Jane Hall has a house full and a handful.

I grin now at another old saying we Jamaicans use when a house is bursting at the seams—especially when the food is scarce: "House full, room full, cyan get a spoonful."

But even with a full house, I know the good Lord is on her side. No child in that district will ever go to bed or to school with a hungry belly so long as Mary Jane Hall draws breath.

I lift my hands to God's blue heaven as I say this: Mary Jane Hall is a good woman.

Now, reader, you know that Mary Jane Hall maintains a household of six. Including herself, there is her husband Joseph Williams—or Tata Joe—her daughter Bernice Bolt and her two girls, Virginia and Lela, and her niece, Lucile.

A seventh member is on the way. Like I said, Bernice's baby could arrive any time now...

2

DECEMBER (1922)

BERNICE VIOLA BOLT

I am not particularly eager to rise from bed this morning—yet, I hardly have a choice. The night has been long, and Yahweh knows I haven't slept well. I'm well past my ninth month now. It is dawn. I slept with the window open, for the cool night breeze offered some relief after another humid tropical day. But sleeping with the window ajar is always an invitation to the creatures I fear most—croaking lizards. I hate the little monsters.

The sun has yet to rise, and already the mongrels are barking, the cockerels crowing in the distance, birds chirping in the trees. These sounds stir me from the land of dreams, though I would rather stay there. Dreams are better than this life. In my dreams, things are soft and bright. In my waking world, each new day is just like the one before.

I open my eyes briefly, then shut them again. I'm not looking forward to another day of the same. I rise, I see about the tea, I go about my chores. That's the rhythm of things. Even in my condition, there's no excuse to lie in bed, not even for a day's rest. But soon there will be change. My child is coming any day now.

I am twenty-four—a young mother. I already have two daughters, and I am confident that this time Yahweh will bless me with a son.

My name is Bernice Viola Bolt—but not for much longer. One day I shall be Mrs. Bernice Wallace. I moved from St. Ann to Clark's Town when I was twelve, along with my mother and her husband, Tata Joe.

It is the child's father who wants a son—not that he doesn't already have others. Still, I wonder why men always place the responsibility of bearing sons upon women. Richard Wallace may have sons, but none share the same mother. He doesn't seem to care. Why should any man care about such things?

But Richard is a good man. A handsome one. And I am determined to give him as many sons as he wants—though only Yahweh alone knows how such things are decided.

I rise now, planting my bare feet on the cold wooden floorboards, catching my breath. It is Christmas morning. All I want is to rest and hope this child makes haste.

I glance at my other two, sleeping soundly, snuggled close to their cousin Lucille at the far end of the bed. Soon, they'll be sleeping next to Ma Jane.

I smile at the sight of them. Virgie is nearly five, and Lela just two—but it's already clear which of the sisters is the stronger. Virgie is calm, gentle. Lela, on the other hand, is fearless. She always manages to get the upper hand. As for Lucille, she may have her way with Virgie at times, but never with little Lela.

Bernice Viola Bolt

IT WAS FINISHED ALMOST AS SOON AS IT BEGAN.

Three days have passed since the birth of my third child. I've delivered two healthy babes before, both long, painful labours. But this little thing slid from my womb so quickly that, by the time the pain struck and my water broke, I barely had time to reach the bed.

I'd been out in the kitchen making tea, a good twenty or thirty paces from the house, when it took me. Tata Joe was already up, tending to the pigs, while Ma Jane sat comfortably on the steps just outside the room she shared with him—smoking her pipe and keeping an eye on everything, as always.

She'd seen me moving about in the kitchen; I could feel her gaze upon me. And somehow, she seemed to know exactly what I'd been thinking. She never trusted Richard. Hardly liked him either. In her opinion, "A bwoy like dat could never be trusted."

I got pregnant just a few months after meeting Richard. We met in Falmouth and fell in love quickly. Too quickly, perhaps. When he first visited our home, Ma Jane didn't even pretend to be polite. She was under the orange tree, puffing away, didn't bother to stand when Richard greeted her. She just looked up at him—tall, strong, towering over her. She grunted with a sly grin and said, "Huh... him a-go breed yuh."

My heart leapt. I turned my gaze away in shame, while Richard—poor thing—took a step back, hands shielding his manhood like his clothes had vanished. Ma Jane always had a way of seeing what was meant to stay hidden. How could she have known I'd already lain with the man?

I found out I was with child just a few weeks after that day. And now, here I lie in bed with my baby girl, born on Christmas Day.

Ma Jane had sent for the midwife the moment my water broke, but by the time the woman arrived, the child had already come. She was tiny, this little thing, and as I looked down at her nursing at my breast, I wondered what to name her.

Richard had been so sure it would be a boy. I thought it best not to ask him to name a daughter.

It was Ma Jane who gave her the name. She stood looking at the child for a long while, then smiled softly and said in that tone of hers—the one that meant her word was final—"Vera." She set her pipe on the table and sat at the edge of the bed. "Likkle V."

Tata Joe stood by the door, grinning like a schoolboy.

"Yuh gwan good, Miss B," he said, clapping his hands as he stepped into the room.

The baby flinched at the sound.

"Clear off! Nuh frighten di pickney," Ma Jane snapped, glancing over her shoulder.

Tata Joe just giggled. In a playful, high-pitched voice he cooed, "Mawnin, Vera. Mawnin, Miss V. Mawnin, Chrismus pickney!" He brought his broad, dark face close to hers, beaming.

3

THE VISIT (FEBRUARY 2011)
VERA

I awoke this morning knowing something was amiss. My caregivers were different. They came to my room far too early and were particularly nice to me—too nice. But as I'm just an old woman of eighty-nine, slowly losing her mind, they likely figured I had no idea what was going on. Little did they know, there's still a bit of wit left in me.

I'm Vera Petrona Wallace. This old, tired body is weak—so weak that sometimes I can hardly stand on the feet God loaned me. I hobble around with my back bent, only because it eases the pain. I'd refused help getting dressed this morning. I can manage that much. Besides, one glance at the girl told me she had no clue how to put herself together, so I saw no reason why she should dress me.

Still, I couldn't make sense of why they were buzzing about like a flock of jancros. Breakfast came on time—too early, even. My room had been swept. The staff was unusually patient. No frowns, no sharp responses to my comments or complaints. Just pleasant smiles and polite "Yes, Miss Vera" and "No, Miss Vera." That's when I knew—someone was coming. It had to be.

Turned out to be one of my seven grandchildren—the youngest

one, the wash belly. And he'd come all the way from Canada to see Granny.

I'd been seated out on the terrace, just by my door, most of the morning. Waiting. Watching. But my eyesight isn't what it once was. I glimpsed figures moving toward me and strained these old brown beads I have for eyes, but they didn't help much.

Then he was before me—my grandson—his arms wrapped around me, his face close to mine. My hands gripped his shoulders as I pushed him back just a bit, needing to see him. I felt the tears welling up as I caught his smile and heard his deep voice.

"Greg?"

"Yes, Granny." He squeezed my hands and gently adjusted my collar, which must've been out of place. Always so careful, always wanting to make sure Granny was presentable.

"Lawd Jesus! Greg?" I could hardly believe it. "Oh God...Greg, yuh cum luk fi Granny?" I wept as he embraced me again, and I studied his face—still my little boy, the one who used to run to the shop for me, stand by my side as I cooked, baked, or made coconut drops.

Later, we sat side-by-side outside my room. There were others with him—the pastor's sons, I think—and one of them had a camera pointed right at me. I said nothing. I had already figured it out.

It was a warm, sunny day. The breeze carried the scent of the sea, and just like that, I was back in the days of my youth.

My grandson held my hand and said he wanted to write about my life. Flo, his mother, had mentioned this before, but now he'd finally come. I didn't know what to tell him, really—my memory, like my eyesight, has started slipping away. I told him I'd do the best I could.

And when he asked his first question, it was as if something opened. The memories came rushing in, like a door flung wide in a hurricane.

Now I lie in bed, unsure what it is I feel. That visit stirred something in me. I delved deep into my past, and for a few hours, I felt alive again—renewed. But it didn't last long. The memories he woke now haunt me.

The days of my youth once felt everlasting. But now... I am old. My sister Lela and I are the only ones left. Still, I smile as a fresh wave of memories floods my mind.

But don't you worry, reader. If I know my grandson—and I believe I do—he'll find his way to Aunt Lala too.

Because like I said... we are the only ones left.

4

SISTERS (1929-1931)

VERA

The sun had yet to show its face, and the small room we all slept in was still as dark as pitch. I could hear the distant crow of a rooster—maybe two, I couldn't tell. But my ears weren't deceiving me; I could hear it. That meant it was almost daylight.

My heart raced as I shifted slightly in my little corner of the bed. I dared not move too suddenly. My sister Lela was a light sleeper, unlike Virgie and Lucille, who Tata Joe always said couldn't wake up even if God's trumpet sounded on Judgment Day. My sisters Lela and Virgie, and my cousin Lucille, all slept in the same bed with me. Lela slept at the edge, Lucille close to the wall, and Virgie and I in the middle.

I hated sleeping next to Lela—she always snored. I would've given anything to have Lucille's spot by the wall. But getting to it meant crawling over everyone, and besides, there were always lizards in the house. We all knew the croaking lizards crawled over the one sleeping against the wall.

Inside our little home, the walls were covered with hundreds of pages from magazines and newspapers—our version of wallpaper back then. As a child, I found this collage of faces, images, and printed words fascinating.

I lay on my stomach, taking long, deep breaths to calm myself. I was only seven, but I knew that by the time the sun swept across the land, I'd be getting a beating from Ma Jane. My heart leapt in my chest, and I could feel the tears welling in my eyes. I had wet the bed. My favorite red and black nightie was soaked through. What was I to do?

But how could I have avoided it? I'd been having one of the best dreams. I was at a party, wearing the prettiest yellow dress. Then I felt the sudden, burning urge to pee. I darted from the house out to the latrine. There was so much food, so much to drink, and when I carefully lifted my dress and started to pee, the relief was the sweetest sensation I'd ever felt.

The dream ended, and I realized I was back in bed, next to my siblings, with a soaking wet mattress beneath me.

I'd hoped the warmth of my body would dry the bed, but it was nearly time for everyone to wake up. I knew Ma Jane was already up. Sometimes I wondered if my granny and Tata Joe ever slept at all.

Then, the familiar click of the radio switch from the adjoining room. Tata Joe was awake. I heard the man on the radio talking about sunshine and a cloudless day for January 5, 1929.

I had little time. I lay there, trying hard to control my sobs. With the sounds of dogs barking and more roosters crowing, I knew the time had come. Ma Jane would beat me for wetting the bed.

Lela, Lucille, and Virgie were already starting to stir, but I leapt from the bed and waited by the door, knowing too well what would happen next.

Sitting up and rubbing sleep from her eyes, Virgie said, "Vera! Yuh piss up di bed!"

Lela glared at me, her frown heavy with frustration. I braced myself, waiting for what I knew would come.

Then, the click of the latch on the door gave me hope. It opened, and I gave Tata Joe a look of thanks before bolting out of the house. My bare feet slipped on the chilly, dewy grass.

She cyan ketch mi, I thought, running faster. I knew I could outrun Lela.

It was always Lela's job to chase and catch me whenever I wet the bed. If she couldn't catch me, Ma Jane would threaten her with the strap. Lela would get the beating for not catching me.

I ran faster at the sound of Ma Jane's voice. "Dis blasted man!"

"Lawd, Miss Mary," Tata Joe laughed. Whenever I wet the bed, he'd always help me by opening the door so I could run away. "Lef di pickney nuh!"

"Nuh badda '*Miss Mary*,' mi, yuh dyam eediat!" Ma Jane's voice cut through the air.

I ran, never looking back, but I could hear Lela calling after me. "Vera! Vera!"

I just kept running. Lela cyan ketch mi, I thought again. She cyan ketch mi…

Vera

LELA GAVE ME MORE CREDIT THAN I DESERVED. AS ANGRY AS SHE WAS, she couldn't deny that I was faster. I was just seven, but my wiry body was light as a bird's feather. Lela, already short of breath, couldn't keep up. It took everything within her not to give up, and she was determined not to take another whipping for me again—Ma Jane's little pet.

We all got our beatings when the time came, but I was the youngest —the wash belly. And with every lash from Granny's strap, every thump to my back, Ma Jane always seemed to feel the pain as much as I did. My crying alone could stop the sun from shining and make the rain fall from the sky. I cried with such despair it sounded worse than the squeals of a pig being butchered out in the yard by Tata Joe. With that sound, no one could help but pity me—even Ma Jane with the strap in her hand.

Lela chased me that morning until I was as tired as an exhausted fowl. I was fast, but I had little endurance, and that's why Lela eventually caught me—not for her speed, but because she slowed down. While I was wiry and frail, Lela was stout and strong. Running for so long took her breath away, but she was patient.

She was gaining on me, and I couldn't help but slow down.

"Vera, Ma Jane call yuh!" Lela shouted.

She shouldn't have said that. As soon as the words left her mouth, I was gone again, darting away like lightning. We raced past Aunt P's house, down the lane, as though the devil and his hosts were after us.

As we passed Aunt P's house, I heard the old woman's shrill encouragement. "Ketch har, Leli!" Aunt P always called Lela by a different name—Leli, that was what the old woman called her.

I ran until I found a place to hide behind some bushes, my chest heaving with sobs, my terror overwhelming. I tried to stifle my cries, but they came uncontrollably. Lela found me there, shaking with fear.

"Cum! Ma Jane call yuh."

"Gweh!" My eyes were wide with terror, but also filled with resolve.

Lela knew I wouldn't go willingly. As soon as she reached for me, I pounced like a wild animal, my red and black nightie now covered in burrs from the bushes. My fingers found her eyes, and I clawed at them with all my might. Lela was strong enough to fend me off, but I fought with everything I had. She dragged me back home with blood smeared across her face.

And from the moment she dragged me through the gate, she knew something had changed. After all the running and the torture of my fingernails scratching at her face, Ma Jane's wrath had subsided. Granny stood there, looking me up and down, her chest heaving with a heavy sigh. She released a playful grunt, the pipe still held between her lips.

"Wah mi a-go do wid yuh, V?" she asked, looking at me fondly. That's what she called me—simply V, or any other pet name she had. "Gwann guh baide, mum."

Just like that, it was done. After everything Lela had endured to bring me back, I was simply let go.

Lela's eyes locked onto mine, full of frustration and anger. Deep down, she knew she couldn't blame me, but her gaze at Ma Jane was laced with rage. Granny's stare, with those sharp green eyes against her pale skin, challenged Lela to say something, just one word. But Lela was determined not to get a beating that morning—not after Ma Jane had let me go for wetting the bed.

As she walked by me, tears still in my eyes, I stuck out my tongue and made a monkey face, feeling the weight of her gaze on me.

Vera

It was Saturday morning, and while Lela, Virgie, and Lucille reluctantly went to the market with Ma Jane, I sat high upon Tata Joe's shoulders, my small hands resting atop his straw hat as we walked in the sun. It was one of the happiest Saturdays of my life—for I was going to Falmouth with him to see my mama, Bernice. A sudden wave of excitement swept over me, and I was sure I'd see my papa too.

Mama had moved to Falmouth long ago, so any chance to visit her was precious.

Tata Joe sang to me as he carried me from Hyde Hall all the way to Falmouth. He was strong and never got tired—never once. That day, I was the happiest girl in Clark's Town, for I'd been allowed to do the thing I loved most in the world: dress up. Nothing mattered more to me than dressing up and singing. Lucille had tied green ribbons in my long plaits to match my dress.

Tata Joe picked up the pace, shifting to a light trot. "Cum on, V," he said. "Cum, wi mekhace."

But all of a sudden, guilt swept over me. I began to cry. I bowed my head until it rested on the top of his hat, wrapping my arms around his neck.

"Cum, V," he said softly. "Nuh cry. Wah mek yuh deh cry?"

"Is Lucille dweet, Tata Joe!" I sobbed, unable to stop myself.

He paused beneath a giant almond tree, its broad canopy casting shade over us. Kneeling down, he rubbed my shoulders and grinned, his eyes bright with kindness. That made it worse. My sisters and I had played a terrible trick on him that morning.

As funny as it was to see Tata Joe run away in fear, I knew we'd been wrong.

"V, nuh worry 'bout Tata Joe," he said, still grinning. "Tata Joe aright."

I couldn't help but grin back. I looked him over—so tall, bigger than most men.

"Tata Joe fraidy-fraidy...but only bull frog mek him fraid."

I started giggling again. The memory of Tata Joe fleeing the house, all of us laughing—including Ma Jane—was just too funny. I never would've guessed he could be scared of anything—well, maybe Ma Jane. But after we found out about his fear of toads, Virgie and Lela made it a game, catching them and tying them to the window.

When Tata Joe saw one, he'd bolt from the house, almost screaming.

"Is one helluva toad," he always said.

Ma Jane would suck her teeth, irritated by the sight of a grown man running from a little toad.

Later, when we reached Falmouth, my mama spent the first hour explaining that she had to work and that we couldn't live with her. Not me. Not the other girls. "Ma Jane response fi unuh," she said.

Just as we were about to leave, my papa arrived. I loved him so much—and he loved me too. I had never seen anyone so tall. He scooped me up in his arms and kissed my face. He tickled me until I screamed with laughter, the sound echoing down the street.

But the joy didn't last long.

It was time to go. I had to leave my mama and papa behind and return home with Tata Joe. They walked with us to the crossroad in Falmouth, where they said goodbye.

And I wept.

Vera

SCHOOL DAYS WERE ALWAYS FUN, BUT I MUCH PREFERRED PLAYING AT home afterward, where I could dress up, comb my hair, and play with my dolly. Best of all were the holidays, when we were often taken to Falmouth to visit our mama.

It was early one Saturday morning. I had been caught in the rain the day before and was now coughing uncontrollably. Unlike my sisters, I was sickly—not as strong as they were. Virgie and Lucille got sick from time to time, but they always bounced back. Lela never got sick. Lela was strong, and she was the only one brave enough to talk back to Ma Jane. But that bravery only lasted until Ma Jane reached for the strap. Still, Lela never seemed to worry about it.

She was the one who protected us at school when older boys or girls tried to bother us. She was the one who ended up fighting in the schoolyard during recess or lunchtime, because she hated to see anyone take advantage of the people she loved. And Lela—as mean and bold as she could be sometimes—loved us. I knew this.

That morning, I sat up in bed, weak as a mangy dog. I could hear the others playing outside, while I lay shut away indoors with a pounding headache and a heavy chest. When the door opened and

Lela walked in with an enamel cup of steaming cerasee tea, I turned my head and started to cry. Cerasee was dreadfully bitter, and as far as I was concerned, I'd rather die than drink it.

"Lela, mi cyan drink it...mi nah drink it!"

Lela wasn't gentle. She was strong. "Open yuh mout," she ordered, grabbing my chin and tilting it up. "Yuh want mi call Ma Jane?" She turned her head as if to call our granny, and I gave in, quickly taking the first sip.

I shut my eyes, coughing again.

"Drink!" she said.

It took several sips and one final gulp to finish the tea, and I fell asleep soon after. But the next morning, I woke up barely able to breathe.

Ma Jane had to hire a car to take me to see Dr. Emdan in Duncans. After taking the medicine he prescribed, I was in such terrible pain I thought I'd die. I began vomiting blood. Amid the sobs and gasps and the awful red chunks coming from my mouth, I could hear my sisters weeping for me.

"Dis man a-go kill mi pickney!" Ma Jane cried. She sent for another car, wrapped me up, and took me back to Duncans in a fury. I was hardly aware of what was happening—but I heard every bitter word Ma Jane uttered.

Dr. Emdan apologized. He had mixed the medicine too strong for a child. It nearly killed me.

By the end of the week, most of my hair had fallen out, and from that day on, I was terrified of medicine. My skinny knees buckled at the sight of a doctor. Dr. Emdan began visiting daily—sometimes twice a day—until I began to feel whole again.

I spent most of my time at home with Ma Jane. I was always sick. Each morning, my sisters would stare at me as they left for school with longing in their eyes—they, too, wanted to stay home and play all day.

One Monday morning, after a weekend of fun and even skipping church the day before, I woke up feeling strong enough to walk my sisters to the crossroad. I wasn't well enough for school, though, and I saw the envy in their eyes. Again, I would get to stay home while they sat in class all day.

"Ma Jane pet!" Lela said, loud enough for the others to hear. She always said that.

I stuck out my tongue—knowing full well Lela hated that most. She gave me a light shove.

"Move an' gweh!" I snapped, already feeling tears rise.

But as soon as Lela, Virgie, and Lucille were out of sight, I missed them.

They were my company.

They were my sisters.

5

LELA GORDON SEPTEMBER 2015
LELA

I t is the month of September, just thirteen days after my ninety-fifth birthday. I am Lela Gordon. When I was young, I was Lela Bolt, though my father's name was Downer. My mother was Bernice Viola Bolt, daughter of old John Bolt, a man I never met. In those days, when an unmarried woman had a child, that child had no right to the father's name.

When I came of age, I took my father's name and became Lela Downer—until I married and took my husband's name. I am the only one left now. My sisters have all gone before me, and only Yahweh knows why he has kept me here this long.

You may wonder why I say Yahweh and not God. In October of 1969, I learned that God is a title, not a name. The Creator's name is Yahweh, and His son is Yeshua. I shared this with my grandnephew Greg, when he came to ask about his grandmother—my sister, Vera. I told him that the one who made the heavens and the earth has a sacred name. Yahweh. Not just "God."

But I am not here to speak of my beliefs. The young man came to ask me to go back more than eighty years in time, and so I tried. His questions were specific, and I did my best to answer, though my memory—like my eyes—has blurred over the years.

Reader, I will try not to bore you. I've lived in this world for ninety-five years, and I have much to tell. The memories of our childhood rose up from the corridors of my mind as if waiting to be summoned. But I won't confuse you. I'll begin at the beginning—with my earliest memories of my little sister, Vera.

6

'DEADLY'

LELA

I can barely remember a time when Vera wasn't sick, and for that reason, she hardly ever left Ma Jane's side. Because she was sickly, Vera was given every ounce of attention. But being unwell never stopped her from dressing up—she adored it. My sisters and I loved to dress up too, but not like Vera. She was meticulous with her appearance. As a child, she was pretty; as a woman, she was beautiful. And since she was our grandmother's favourite, I often teased her, calling her Ma Jane's little pearl—because, in truth, there were times Vera could do no wrong in Ma Jane's eyes. And believe me, she knew how to use that to her advantage.

To me, she was Ma Jane's pearl, but to one Mr. Freighter from upper Trelawny, she was Deadly. That's what he called her, and it stuck. The name fit, too—because Vera was always sick, always being rushed to the doctor, always laid up in bed. From the moment Mr. Freighter gave her that name, Deadly became her nickname.

There was one reason in particular the name felt so fitting. Back then, we went to church every Sunday—like clockwork. Ma Jane made sure we were up early, finished our chores, broke our fasts, and got dressed for service. As always, Vera took great pride in getting ready. But for months, the strangest thing kept happening. Every Sunday, like

25

clockwork, Vera fainted—right there in church. And every Sunday, we'd leave church because of it. Yet as soon as we got home, she was fine again—laughing, playing, as if nothing had happened.

Ma Jane and Tata Joe were baffled, until one Easter Sunday, the mystery was solved.

The whole family had gone to Saint Michael's Anglican Church, a grand old stone building that stood near the main road, not far from the market. The bell tower loomed large to us children, and when it rang, it echoed so loud it felt like it could wake the dead. The graveyard around the church was filled with old tombstones we could hardly bear to look at.

That morning, the church was packed. The sound of the organ filled the space, and sunlight poured through the stained-glass windows, casting colours across the pews. Tata Joe had warned Virgie, Lucille, and me: Watch Vera from the moment we walk in. And so we did.

Vera sat between Ma Jane and Tata Joe, and we kept our eyes on her as the pews filled up and the procession began. In those days, the white folks had their own pews near the front—those weren't for us. Just as an old white man, Mr. Krueger Milliner, made his way past us to his seat, Vera gasped softly. Her eyes bulged, her body trembled—and then, like clockwork, she fainted.

That was the moment we finally understood: it was the old man's beard. Mr. Milliner had a long, white beard that hung down to his waist, and Vera was terrified of it.

After that, Vera stayed home whenever Mr. Milliner went to church. "Mi fraid," she'd whisper as she got dressed. So Ma Jane would send me ahead to see if the bearded man was there before Vera came.

Vera's fear of long white beards became something we used—especially when it was time for her to take medicine. She hated the taste of cerasee tea. I'd hold out the cup and say, "Mi a-go call Joe Bachos," the old man down the road with the same long white beard. At just the mention of his name, Vera gulped the bitter tea down without a word.

Lela

OUR DAYS AT SCHOOL WERE WONDERFUL, AND AS EVERYONE KNEW THAT Lela Bolt loved to romp and was fearless, I used that reputation to protect my sisters. No other boy or girl, no matter how big, could mistreat my family. As I did at home, I watched over Virgie, Lucille, and Vera. I had the strength and the will, and was usually involved in fights on the school grounds. Mind you, I'm not saying I was a bully—I simply was never one to turn the other cheek. But don't worry, I'm ninety-five now. Yahweh and the years have softened me plenty. Still, I wasn't easy back then—not easy at all.

There's one incident I remember clearly—the day I taught my older sister Virgie a lesson she never forgot. But first, let me explain how things were in Ma Jane's household. Our grandmother was loving, but she was also very strict. She was a good woman, and I must say she brought us up well. Much of her knowledge was passed down and helped shape the lives we later led. As children, though, we were blind to the fact that those little punishments were indeed for our own good.

Vera, as I've mentioned before, was Ma Jane's pearl. She feared Ma Jane, but not as much as Lucille and Virgie. As for myself, I respected Ma Jane, but I never feared her. She knew this, and I was sure each time she looked at me—especially when I talked back—she saw herself within me. Like Ma Jane, I was strong, but she was the matriarch, not Lela Bolt. That, I had to learn the hard way. But let's not rush ahead—for that's an entirely different story. We'll get to one of the most important lessons I learned from Ma Jane soon enough.

Ma Jane was a very busy woman. She was a healer who knew nearly everything about herbs. As young as I was, and though not the eldest, I was the one who ended up doing Ma Jane's work when she was out. If she wasn't shopping at the market, she was off visiting the sick. And I—the unwilling apprentice—was left to treat children with cuts and sores. I can't count how many sore feet I washed and dressed as a child, how many festering wounds I had to clean, or scabs I had to cut away. It was a bloody and smelly job, and I cannot say I enjoyed it. But it earned Ma Jane much respect.

My grandmother was so strong—so strict—that parents brought their children to her for a good flogging. She didn't need to know what the flogging was for, nor did she care. So if I wasn't busy cleaning sore feet, my sisters and I were entertained by watching our school friends get a proper beating from Ma Jane. She couldn't stand seeing us with any child she considered rude or disrespectful. We weren't allowed to play with any child she disliked. Her word was final.

"Come inna di yard," she'd say whenever she spotted us with someone she didn't approve of.

Now, don't think I've forgotten about the lesson I taught Virgie— I'm getting there. Remember, I've just turned ninety-five.

Ma Jane wasn't just a healer and district disciplinarian—she was the best cook around. Give her any two ingredients and she'd make a belly-filling meal. And being the kind woman she was, all children were welcome at her table. She had a big black pot with two handles that looked like arms akimbo. Most folks called them *kimbo pots*, but I called Ma Jane's an *elbow pot*. All the children were fed from that elbow pot.

On schooldays, we would walk home for lunch, since Clark's Town Primary was just a short distance away. We loved our lunches, and Ma Jane would leave them covered on the table before heading out for the day. But for months, Virgie had been playing a cruel trick on me—and I finally decided to teach her a lesson.

Maybe she did it because she and Lucille were close, and Vera was the youngest and would cry all day until Ma Jane returned. But after days of planning, I made sure Virgie would never trifle with me again. I'm not proud of what I did—but we were children.

Virgie made sure to run home ahead of everyone at lunchtime. I wasn't in a rush, since I loved to romp on the school grounds and stop along the way. But each day, when I got home, I noticed someone had eaten part of my lunch.

"Who eat mi lunch?" I asked Lucille. Not a word. I turned to Vera, and saw fear in her eyes.

"Who trouble mi lunch, Deadly?"

Vera cringed at the sound of her nickname.

"A nuh mi," she said. "Ah Virgie!"

Virgie had already gone back to school with her full portion—and half of mine.

So I prepared to get her. I warned Lucille and Vera not to say a word, or they'd get worse. The next day, I went to Mr. Nezbit's shop and took a big package of sweet biscuits and a cool drink—on trust. I told him to put it on Ma Jane's tab, knowing full well I'd get a beating. But I'd decided the day before that the beating was worth it.

I filled my belly with biscuits and drink, then headed home early for lunch. Tata Joe raised pigs, and at the back of the house was the pigpen, where we'd dump food scraps—the *crawl*, we called it. When Virgie came home and walked toward the table for her lunch, I took both plates—hers and mine—and marched straight to the pigpen. I dumped both lunches into the crawl.

Virgie gasped, shocked, and didn't dare do anything. That day, she went back to school with a hungry belly. She wouldn't dare trust anything from Mr. Nezbit's shop—none of us would, out of fear of Ma Jane's flogging. I returned to school content, while Virgie went back hungry.

Later that evening, Ma Jane came home from the shop. I got a beating. But so did Virgie. She hadn't had the courage to go to the shop and get something to eat on trust. So I told her, plain and simple—she should've done what I did. At least she would've been flogged with a full belly.

7

THE 'JOSEPH' OF THE FAMILY
VERA

Our childhood days were filled with such fun, though for me
—the one everyone called Deadly—it was a time marked
by discomfort and pain. I think of those days now and lift
my hands, thanking God for keeping me alive.

By the time I was sixteen, much had changed. The days of playing
dolly-house with my sisters out in the yard among the trees were long
gone. Lela, Virgie, Lucille, and I would collect humongous palm leaves
from the coconut trees and use them to build our house. Within that
haven, shaded from the hot Jamaica sun, we could hear the happy
birds sing. But by the time I was a teenager, those days—and my
frequent sicknesses—were behind me. I was proud to have shed the
name "Deadly" as I emerged into adolescence. Nearly everything had
changed, except for one thing: I was still Ma Jane's favourite—or as
Lela and Lucille always said, "Ma Jane's pearl."

Much changed the year I turned sixteen, but even before then, after
the days of dolls and being sick were gone, I realized I was different.
The days when Ma Jane would smile at me with that pipe between her
lips, puffing smoke from her nostrils as she watched me climb atop the
old rusty kerosene pan to wash her long coat—those days were gone. I
did everything to help Ma Jane around the house, and for that, she

cherished me. Lela, Lucille, and Virgie said I was her pet, but I'd earned it.

I remember one evening at home with my sisters. I must have been fifteen. We were all seated on the steps of the old board house. It had been a long day for Ma Jane, and as she walked through the gate, she looked at us all before casting her gaze toward the sky.

"Rain deh cum," she said.

She didn't need to ask us to grab the clothes from the line—her look alone questioned why we hadn't already noticed the dark clouds in the distance. I was the first to move toward the clothes, humming as I tossed each garment into the washpan.

Several boys passed by, and I hadn't noticed they had stopped to watch me until Ma Jane called after them.

"Clear off from mi gate!" she said.

But one boy still called out, "Vera! Vera!"—and then he was gone.

Ma Jane tapped the ashes from her pipe into her palm and tossed them into her mouth, her usual habit. Her green eyes seemed to pierce right through me, as if she knew what I'd been thinking.

"V, chubble nuh set like rain," she said. "Di bwoy nuh have no ambition. 'Im is a cruff."

Ma Jane had seen it before I even realized I was becoming a woman.

It was Lela who first made me realize how much we'd all changed and grown up. She was eighteen then. While I busied myself with dressing up and keeping up with the latest hairstyles, my sister was listening to the radio, always showing interest in politics. In 1938, there were serious riots due to unemployment, and there was much resentment toward British racial policies. Lela supported the People's National Party, founded by Norman Manley. The days of playing with dolls were done.

Ma Jane also knew things had changed. Her four girls had grown, but she refused to relinquish her matriarchal power. She complained constantly about our love for dressing up and going to dances. She was especially disappointed in me—her pet. For as much as Lucille and Lela loved to dance, I loved it more. Virgie hated to dance with others, so she alone obeyed Ma Jane's command to stay away from the dances.

I couldn't stay away. I had fallen in love with the way the men looked at me. I welcomed the sudden pause on the dance floor—the way they froze when I walked into the hall. I loved how they gazed at me while still holding their own women, and I even enjoyed the scathing looks from those women. I revelled in the power I held over their men. I was as poor as every other girl at the dances, but I knew I was one of the prettiest.

I would get my hair done the day before a dance, and my sisters did the same. We didn't dare sleep lying down that night—we wouldn't risk ruining the hairdos. Sleeping upright was our only option. I used a sweet-smelling product in my hair called *Black and White*. Lela used to tease me, saying she could always tell when I was coming, because she'd smell the *Black and White* long before I arrived—and after I'd left.

The dances were the most amazing events of our youth. We danced to live music—full orchestras with saxophones, trumpets, banjos, drums, even flutes. Donald Blake, a saxophonist, was like a brother to us. His mother had died when he was young, and Ma Jane had taken care of him. She didn't like it much, but Donald often came by with his saxophone so we could practice dancing. Lela danced. I danced. Lucille danced. Virgie wanted nothing to do with it.

As for me—I made sure I looked my best, because I did dance the best. I always won the contests. It was a usual request that I perform on stage, and I felt free, my happiest, when I sang and danced.

I was devastated when Donald died. It was late at night, just days into the new year of 1940. He had walked us home in the dark after a party, and although we were exhausted from dancing, we were joyful. The dark sky was lit with stars, the moon was full, and we could hear our laughter echo through the night. Lela had insisted there was no need for Donald to walk us home, for she was never afraid. But Lucille and I welcomed the company.

Donald took the shortcut through the field to get home—he lived at Long Pond, near Clark's Town's sugar factory. By morning, the news had come: Donald's house had caught fire in the night. He'd died in his sleep.

I wept for days. We would never see our brother and friend again, nor hear the beautiful notes from his saxophone...

———————

———————

———————

Lela

EVERYONE KNEW VERA WAS THE BEST DANCER. MY SISTER WAS LIKE A magnet—she made friends as easily as fish took to water, but she never kept them for long. Vera was naturally drawn to young men, just as they were to her, and cared very little that these friendships often led to conflict, especially with other girls who saw her as a threat. But hate her as they might, they could do nothing—and they never dared speak a word against her in my presence. Everyone knew better than to cross Lela Downer.

It was mid-September, just after my twentieth birthday. I'd finished school and found a job that paid little, but it gave me independence. That weekend, Vera, Lucille, and I went to a dance—our first after the long, aching months since Donald Blake's death in the fire. My sister had cried for weeks, even vowed never to go dancing again. Donald was gone. But Vera's vow was short-lived. With her love for singing and dancing, nothing could keep her from the parties for long.

She was just months away from her seventeenth birthday, and we couldn't wait for that September night. The three of us—Lucille, Vera, and I—told ourselves we were going in Donald's honour, that we were celebrating his memory after all he'd taught us. I could still hear Donald's saxophone blaring, see him tapping his feet, his muscular frame swaying as he coached Lucille and me through the steps. Vera never needed the help—she never placed a foot wrong.

The evening breeze was cool and carried the sweet fragrance of the lady of the night plant. As we dressed, we heard Ma Jane's voice cutting through the night air. She never approved of us going out late.

"Dem dress up lakka street gal, di tree ah dem."

Vera and Lucille flinched. I scowled. We could hear our older sister Virgie chiming in from the other room.

"Mi nuh know wah dem si inna all dat, Ma Jane. Vera an Lucille falla everything Lela do. Everyweh Lela guh mi si dem deh."

Ma Jane agreed. "Dem ah worlian."

I made for the door, furious, ready to confront Virgie for her mouth. She knew she was wrong. Vera, Lucille, and I loved the dances for no other reason than the fun of it. I wasn't leading them astray.

"Lela," Lucille begged, grabbing my arm, "Nuh badda wid har...leff har."

I said, "Is wah wrong wid she?" Vera and Lucille had to restrain me.

We left through the gate with Ma Jane still quarrelling behind us. As we walked down the lane, Vera lagged behind, for nothing pained her more than disappointing Ma Jane. But the guilt didn't last. As we neared the hall, the sound of the orchestra floated toward us, and Vera surged ahead, humming at first, then singing Lionel Belasco's popular tune:

"Oh my Rufus, hold me tight...

Oh squeeze me with all your might..."

Her waist was tiny and her hips swayed as she skipped along, her loyalty to Ma Jane already forgotten.

She entered the hall ahead of us, as always. The night usually belonged to Vera—dancing with any fellow brave enough to defy his girl and ask her to the floor. They couldn't resist her: the way she moved, the way she looked at them—wordless commands in her eyes that made them forget all else. Vera knew the power she held over men. What she didn't understand was what happens when you play with fire.

Lucille and I tired after the third hour on our feet. Our legs ached, and we sat down to rest. But Vera kept going, tireless, right up until the moment she found herself in the middle of a brawl.

It didn't matter who started it. All I saw was another woman with her hands on my sister, her man nearby trying to pull them apart. Vera clawed at the girl's face. The music stopped. My feet no longer hurt, and I didn't even feel it when I struck the woman. She hit the ground. Her man pushed Vera aside and stepped toward me—but before he could lay a hand on me, I hit him square in the face.

Yes, I fought men. I seldom lost.

I didn't lose that night.

We walked home early the next morning. Vera fussed over her torn dress. My knuckles were bloody and my lip split. Between my face and Vera's disheveled look, Ma Jane quarrelled through the entire day. And from then on, dances were strictly forbidden.

Lela

BY CHRISTMAS OF THAT YEAR, MUCH HAD CHANGED.

Vera, Lucille, Virgie—and even I—had obeyed Ma Jane's command to stay home on Friday and Saturday nights. Since that night in September, we'd kept to the house, heedful of her words. But Christmas parties were always the best, and missing those dances was unbearable. That weekend, after weeks of boredom, I decided enough was enough. I was a grown woman of twenty.

I told myself Ma Jane was a hypocrite. Surely, she had gone dancing in her youth. She was seventy-one now, still strong despite the chest pains she often complained about. She still smoked heavily, still had the odd habit of eating ashes from her pipe. Vera often begged her to stop, but our granny was as stubborn as ever—and still to be feared. She no longer used the strap, but we all, Vera, Lucille, Virgie, and I, obeyed her without question.

That Christmas Eve, I decided I was done asking permission.

Vera and Lucille pleaded with me to stay, but I was firm.

I would go to the dance.

And that decision changed my life.

I dressed in my best that night, proud and defiant. It was 1940, and I stepped through the gate expecting Ma Jane to call me back, curse me, something. But she said nothing. Just grunted as I passed. I didn't look back.

At the dance, I felt triumphant. Independent. My sisters weren't there, and for once, I danced without worry or judgment. I danced until I couldn't dance anymore.

By dawn, I returned home.

I saw the soft glow of the lamp through the window.

Ma Jane and Tata Joe were sitting on the steps on their side of the house. Their voices, sharp and rising, silenced as soon as I walked through the gate. They had been arguing.

To my surprise, my sisters were also awake. One by one, they came into the yard.

"Unuh gwaan back inna di house," Ma Jane snapped.

Virgie went in first. Vera and Lucille followed.

"Mawnin, Ma Jane...mawnin, Tata Joe."

I kept my eyes on them both.

Ma Jane's pipe hung to one side of her mouth. Smoke drifted from her nostrils.

Tata Joe's eyes were full of sorrow. He looked at her, then shook his head.

"Miss Mary, mi seh—"

"Luk yah, man! Kibba yuh mouth!" she barked.

She wouldn't be challenged. Her emerald eyes stayed locked on me.

She motioned toward a small bag by the gate.

"Nuh come inna mi yawd," she said.

"Since yuh ah big woman, nuh come back inna mi house."

I saw it in her eyes.

She'd made her decision the moment I stepped out the night before.

It was Christmas morning. Vera's birthday.

I could hear her weeping inside.

And by Yahweh, I wanted to weep too.

I wanted to fall at Ma Jane's feet, beg for forgiveness, plead for another chance.

But the look in her eyes told me not to bother.

I wouldn't let her see me cry.

I wouldn't let her see my fear.

Though I hadn't the faintest idea where I would go, I picked up the bag and walked away.

I left the only home I'd ever known, wondering if things would've gone differently had it been Vera who defied her.

I was certain my sister would've been forgiven.

I wasn't.

Lela

YAHWEH MOVES IN MYSTERIOUS WAYS.

I was already in tears by the time I passed the first few houses down the lane, silently weeping. As I approached Aunt P's house, I felt a sudden urge to speak with her. I knew she loved me—she had always been a source of comfort and good advice.

Aunt P used to say she'd known my father, a shoemaker. She'd

37

always admired how respectful and well-mannered he was. And she'd always called me *Leli*.

Her son Albert brought me into her bedroom. The old woman lay resting, but when she saw me, she raised her head and beckoned me closer.

"Whaap'm, Leli?"

Her voice was soft, kind.

I dropped my bag to the floor and sat at the edge of her bed. My head shook slowly, still in disbelief, still unable to speak. I let out a soft sob, then another, until the tears took over. The words wouldn't come. My chest tightened with grief.

Eventually, I managed to explain what had happened—that Ma Jane had turned me out.

"Mi nuh know whey mi a-go guh, Aunt P."

"Nuh cry, Leli," she said gently.

Aunt P was a godly woman. Her voice, soothing as a hymn, calmed something in me.

"Don't cry. One day, you will be the Joseph of your family."

I didn't know what she meant—and I didn't ask.

But something about the way she said it stayed with me.

I never left Aunt P's house that day. She insisted I rent one of the spare rooms—one shilling and twopence a month. And I agreed. Right then and there, I vowed that Ma Jane would never get the chance to put me out again.

I took the first help I was given.

And I started my life on my own.

8

MY ONE CHILD
VERA

By the time I was twenty, much had changed in our household. Shortly after Ma Jane put Lela out, Virgie left too, choosing to live with our mother in Falmouth. I found myself lonely, longing for the days when the four of us girls lived under one roof. I missed how Ma Jane's cooking would draw us all to the table. I missed the way Tata Joe's jokes could set us all laughing—how even Ma Jane couldn't resist his banter.

Lucille was on the verge of starting her own life. Like Lela and Virgie, she had found herself a man. She was happy, mostly, though they quarrelled for hours on end. During those years, I often wondered why I was the one who couldn't find a good, faithful man.

My first job was with the Chinaman, Alfred Williams, as a general cleaner. I would later become one of the most sought-after employees among the prominent Chinese families who owned many of the businesses in Clark's Town. The large stores, bakeries, and groceries were all run by them. I nursed their children, cooked, cleaned. I worked with Miss Chin and Oswald Chin. I also worked for Miss May, helping care for her three children.

I was young and full of energy, so I took every opportunity that came. I worked for Eva Anderson too—she owned one of Clark's

Town's clothing stores. Miss Eva sold everything from books and school supplies to sweets. She had even started the town's only private pre-school. The woman was good to me. Miss Eva was short and fair-skinned—one might've mistaken her for white.

Not long after Lela left, I must have been nearly nineteen when I became pregnant. Ma Jane was not pleased, but I was grown. Soon I was heavy with child. My days of dancing and parties were mostly behind me—though I still managed to go out now and then, even if Ma Jane didn't like it.

I was five or six months along when that fool cost me my child's life. I cannot remember his name, but he had always teased me, even before I was with child. I never liked him—the fool. Wherever he saw me, he'd bother me, sometimes walking close behind and calling out, "Vera! Vera!"

I never once answered him. In my eyes, he didn't exist.

One afternoon, I was walking home from Oswald Chin's shop when I heard him again—his voice before I even saw him.

"Vera, pretty Vera," he called.

"Clear off!" I said, and tried to pass him.

"Mek mi carry yuh bag fi yuh, pretty Vera!"

He smiled like he always did. I still don't know why I hated him so. Then he reached out and touched me. Rage flooded through me. With my grocery bag in one hand and my swollen belly in front of me, I bent to grab a rock to fling at him.

I fell—hard.

And all he did that day was laugh.

I thought I was fine afterward. I went about my business. But within a few days, I was in terrible pain. I had no idea my child had died. I bled badly. Even with Ma Jane's help, I believed the baby would be fine.

But pushing a dead child from my body days later...

That was one of the worst pains of my life.

I lost another baby the following year. After that, I came to believe that not only would I be without a good man...

I would also be childless.

———————

———————

———————

Vera

I ALWAYS ADMIRED A MAN WHO KNEW HIS MUSIC AND WAS LIGHT ON HIS feet, for I loved to sing and dance. Most people never knew the fathers of my first two children—the ones I lost. I still think of that fool who made me fall and lose my first child. My heart aches even now. That child's father would've been proud—he was a musician.

The second baby I lost was fathered by a Chinaman. God alone knows why I lost them both.

When I met Rupert Barrett at a party one night, I fell in love instantly. He was one of Clark's Town's best musicians—and could he dance! I found him a little short for my liking, but "Tutu" Barrett, as they called him, knew how to keep up with a lady on the dance floor. He could play his banjo all night long, only ever stopping to dance with me. He was a shoemaker by trade.

I had watched him for some time, and he watched me. It was said Tutu preferred big, fat women—but I wasn't fat. I'd watch him dance with those women, and he knew I was watching. It made me laugh sometimes, seeing this little man clutched in the arms of a large woman. But don't be fooled—no matter the size of his partner, Tutu always held his own.

When he finally got the nerve to ask me for a dance, I made sure he'd never feel the need to dance with another—big or small. I'd fallen for him, you see. And love makes us blind. I'd always fooled myself into thinking I could change a man, mold him into what I wanted. I was certain Tutu loved me. But he was still a man.

Because of our shared love of music, Tutu always tried to teach me the banjo. But I could never learn it—my fingers would ache after just a few tries.

"Ih easy, Vera," he'd say, sometimes getting frustrated when I struck the wrong note.

"Mi cyan learn di blasted thing," I told him.

We had an agreement: he'd play, and I would sing.

Tutu lived with his uncle, Sammy Reid. A few months after we began courting, I was pregnant again. I prayed to God I wouldn't lose this baby—not a third time. By the seventh month, my belly was so swollen I was sure I was carrying twins.

Tutu and I were no longer together then. He'd had the nerve to say the child wasn't his. That hurt. I loved him. But Tutu was not a one-woman man. I found myself at the centre of many quarrels over that handsome little shoemaker. He had children with two other women I knew well—Miss Francis and Miss Madeline.

My child would end up with many siblings—Tutu Barrett had ten children.

I gave birth to a baby girl on July 10th, 1943. I was twenty-one and couldn't have been happier. She was beautiful. I named her Flora.

Ma Jane was seventy-four, but still strong. She helped in the early days of Flo's life, especially when the baby fell sick just days after she was born. I looked to my granny, weeping.

"Wah mi a-go duh, Ma Jane...wah mi a-go duh?"

"Nuh worry yuhself," she said.

It was Sammy Reid, Tutu's uncle, who helped the child. He came every Sunday, took Flo with him, and fed her until she got better. She wouldn't take to my breast, but Sammy got her to eat. I never forgot that man's kindness.

As for Tutu Barrett—the same man who once claimed she wasn't his—he was proud of her. Flo was beautiful. I still smile remembering his voice. He stuttered sometimes. He'd show her off, beaming.

"Is...is...is m-my pretty dawta dis," he'd say.

"Ma...ma...my pretty dawta..."

Tutu loved his children, but he wasn't always present. And even though he was a shoemaker, I used to think Flo would have all the shoes in the world. She never got a single pair.

I was mother and father. But with work keeping me busy, it fell to Ma Jane to raise Flo. We all lived together. Ma Jane was old, but she remained the head of our family—raising not just her children, but her grandchildren, and now her great-grandchild. Three generations under one roof.

<hr>

<hr>

<hr>

Vera

I WAS NEVER ONE TO HANDLE THE DEATH OF LOVED ONES WELL, AND WHEN my father passed away, it broke me—for he was so young. Papa died long before Flo was born. Along with his name, Papa left me brothers, and my favourite was Lester Wallace. Lester had moved to England years after Papa died, but we were always in touch. A letter from Lester always brought me joy.

Flo had grown into a lovely little girl. Left in Ma Jane's care while I worked, my girl flourished. I'll admit, it was best that she was raised by Ma Jane, for my life was hectic. As a child, Flo was studious and obedient—every child had to be when living with my granny, Mary Jane Hall. Tata Joe and Ma Jane were a blessing; I couldn't have raised the child without them.

I can't recall anyone who didn't love my daughter. Flo was beautiful, a tiny little thing. Her hair cascaded down her back, and because she was so slender, someone had nicknamed her *Ants Picker*—the Jamaican name for the arrow-headed warbler, a petite, beautiful bird.

It wasn't easy affording things, but with the work I did for the

Chinese and Miss Eva Anderson, I managed to give Flo what she needed. Every now and then, I'd buy her a little dress... a new pair of shoes. I wouldn't have my child walk to school barefoot. I even managed to pay for her organ lessons.

I always took the child to see her father. Though he was hardly around, Flo loved him, and Tutu—ever the show-off—loved her dearly. I remember one day at the market. Flo and I were walking when we saw Tutu there with several of his friends. As I said, Flo had many siblings from her father's side—between myself, Francis, and Madeline, Tutu must've had seven or more children. He was short in stature, but the ladies adored him just as much as his children did.

Even before we saw him, I heard his loud voice—boasting, as usual, about his children.

At the sound of her father's voice, Flo's eyes lit up. She looked up at me, ready to run to him. I held my tongue, though I wanted to call him a blasted boaster.

"Yuh... yuh... yuh si har deh? Is mi dawta, yuh know... Cum... si mi dawta dem..."

By the time we reached him and saw Flo's sisters all around him, I'd already lost patience. Tutu and I were civil, but I'd been angry for years—ever since he'd claimed Flo wasn't his. The nerve of him. Yet still, his stammering continued:

"An mi hab some prettier one deh 'bout..."

Then he saw her. His eyes lifted and lit up when they landed on Flo. He spread his arms wide.

"Si deh! Wah mi tell yuh? Si mi pretty dawta, Flo!"

Flo sprang into his lap, grinning wide as he presented her to his friends.

"My pretty dawta dis! Yuh si har? Is mi dawta!"

I walked up, head held high, and gave a curt nod.

"Missah Barrett," I said, fingers laced before me.

Tutu began to sing.

"My beautiful Veeeraaa..."

I grabbed my hanky and covered my face, laughing in spite of myself. The little fool always knew how to make me smile.

"Veeeraa, Vera, I love you..." he crooned, tilting his head back, Flo still perched on his lap.

"All right, Missah Barrett," I said. I never doubted his love for me, but Tutu Barrett had not been good to me.

He came to the house later that evening to see Flo. The two adored each other, and while they visited, Ma Jane, Tata Joe, and I observed. When he came to say goodbye, he looked at Ma Jane with a sly grin.

"All right, Miss Mary."

Ma Jane turned her head and puffed on her pipe, emerald eyes dulling behind her silver-rimmed spectacles. She grunted and said nothing.

Flo received her last hugs, always smiling for her papa.

"All right," said Tutu. "Is my pretty gal dis... my pretty dawta!"

Ma Jane could hold her tongue no longer.

"Caca faat! Bwoy, yuh deh chat 'bout 'my pretty gal'—when last yuh bring har one shilling or so?"

Tutu Barrett made a very quick exit as soon as Ma Jane started.

9

BUSHA EARL
LELA

Being Vera's big sister had never been easy. In fact, Virgie was the eldest, not me. But my older sister was quiet, seldom got angry, and tried her hardest to please Ma Jane. Our granny loved us all, but if Virgie ever thought obedience would bring her closer to Ma Jane, she was wrong—for it was Vera who was the favourite.

I was never sure if Vera knew how special she was to our granny. She'd been coddled by all of us since she was sickly as a child. But one thing I can say for certain is that my sister took a lot for granted. And I, Lela, was always the one left to set things right.

The day Ma Jane turned me out of the house, I swore I'd never again be dependent on anyone. I was angry then—furious, really—but looking back, I can see she did me a favour. My life would've gone another way if she hadn't put me out that Christmas morning.

I went to stay with Aunt P and stayed as long as I needed. I worked hard, saved harder. A few years later, I owned my own bar in Falmouth.

Back then, it wasn't easy being a woman running a bar. But I was strong. I fought if I had to—and it was never my intention to lose, no matter who stood in front of me. Everyone who stepped into my bar knew: Lela Downer wasn't an easy woman.

I missed my family, but life had pushed us all in different directions. Lucille and her Charles were building a life together and talked of marriage. Virgie had found a man, too, though she still lived in Falmouth with our mother. I had found someone as well—though I can't say things were good. In fact, I can hardly bear to speak his name, for that man brought nothing but trouble into my life.

They called him Busha Earl.

I'd always been fearless, always strong. I'd fought many men just to protect Vera—my baby sister with a habit of falling for the wrong ones. She couldn't help it. Men were drawn to her beauty, and more often than not, they ended up mistreating her. And if there was one thing I couldn't stand, it was seeing my sisters hurt.

But I can admit, the one man I ever truly feared was Busha Earl. Only Yahweh knows why I ever thought I loved him.

Busha liked to hit his women. But I always fought back.

I believe some things in life happen for a reason. To teach us. To reveal who we are. And when Busha Earl came into my life—and later left it—I came out the other side a stronger woman. Ten times stronger.

My niece Flo must have been seven or eight when Busha Earl came around. I visited Clark's Town often to see my family—but if I'm honest, those visits became more frequent for another reason.

Busha Earl was a cheating man. And that was something I refused to tolerate.

So, more often than not, I took matters into my own hands...

———————

———————

———————

Flora

47

I can hardly recall Mama ever spanking me as a child. Though we lived in the same household, it was my great-grandmother, Ma Jane, who governed it.

By the time I turned seven, Ma Jane was already in her eighties, but she was strong—ever puffing on her pipe and eating the ashes when she was done. She would tap the still-warm ashes into the palm of her hand and toss them into her mouth.

She simply called me Flo. Our mum—she pronounced it *Moom*. While others called me Ants Picker because of my tiny body and long hair, Ma Jane always stuck with Flo or just *mum*.

My aunts, Virgie and Lucille, always said Ma Jane loved me as much as she loved my mama. But Aunt Lela? She would just shake her head and say, "Vera ah Ma Jane pet."

Aunt Lela was a solid, stout woman. She may not have known it, but for many years, I lived in fear of her. She was bold, direct—the only one who ever dared to tell Ma Jane when she was wrong. No one else had the courage.

Ma Jane was old, but she was a stubborn woman. I know she loved me, just as Tata Joe did, but she ruled the household with a firm hand. If she believed I'd done something wrong, there was no explaining it away, no convincing her otherwise. Only Aunt Lela could've stood up to her.

Ma Jane expected me to be home on time after school. And whenever she decided I needed a flogging, not even Mama could save me.

My walk to school wasn't far. The streets of Clark's Town bustled with cars, bicycles, people on foot—sometimes even donkeys. I loved walking in the cool morning sun. But by midday, the island blazed hot, and we spent our recesses and lunch breaks beneath the wide shade of the big trees. That was life at seven years old, in 1950.

Clark's Town Primary School sat on a large stretch of land just past the market at the crossroad. Every morning, we gathered at the front gate for devotion, the air full of chatter and laughter, rows of children from grade one to six.

Each school day began the same way—our principal standing in front of us, teachers monitoring their classes. The latecomers, lined up off to the side, would wait for a flogging after the singing and the Lord's Prayer.

Our teacher had divided the class into three groups. At the end of each day, one group stayed behind to tidy the classroom. One particular afternoon, it was my group's turn. I stayed behind, helping my classmates straighten desks and sweep the floor. We were nearly done when we finally left together.

Just as we passed the market, I saw Ma Jane coming.

She was walking briskly, her silver spectacles sliding down her nose, a strap clutched in her hand.

"Flo," one of my friends whispered, "Miss Mary deh cum!"

I knew what would happen next. There was no point trying to explain why I hadn't made it home on time.

Ma Jane whipped me right there in the street. Then she sent me to walk ahead of her, scolding me the whole way home for staying back to play with friends.

"Yuh think yuh cum ah school fi romp?" she barked.

She talked the entire way home. I walked and cried, burning with shame and embarrassment.

Flora

BY THE TIME MA JANE AND I ARRIVED HOME, MY TEARS AND SOBS HAD come to an end, but I still walked ahead of her without uttering a word.

Mama and Tata Joe were sitting with Aunt Lela on the veranda, deep in conversation. Like a well-mannered girl, I offered a polite Good afternoon, eyes wide with fear as I looked at Aunt Lela. She was always in a temper, always telling people what she didn't like and what she wouldn't put up with. But that day, when I looked into her eyes, I saw something else—something mingled with her usual boldness.

It was fear.

And if Aunt Lela was afraid, then I—little Ants Picker—ought to be terrified.

I knew better than to interrupt grown folks talking. That alone could earn me another flogging. So I went about my business quietly, but my ears stayed open. What I heard wasn't good at all. Aunt Lela had gotten herself into serious trouble. Mass Busha Earl was angry, and he was expected to come to our house because of what she'd done.

I started on my chores. Every child, especially girls, had to make themselves useful. As I fetched rainwater from the large drum beside the house, I overheard more of the story.

"Mi kraw out har eye dem," Aunt Lela said.

Mama burst into a high-pitched laugh and leaned forward. "Kiss mi neck!" she exclaimed as Lela described what she'd done to Miss Trulie when she found out Busha Earl had been seeing the woman.

Aunt Lela slapped her chest. "Im have sum nerve, keepin' woman wid mi."

Ma Jane puffed her pipe. Tata Joe stood quietly behind her.

"Yuh wrong, Lela," said Ma Jane.

"Mi nuh kya," Aunt Lela replied, showing no remorse at all.

I knew Miss Trulie—she was a fat woman—and I'd overheard that she'd been having an affair with Aunt Lela's man. When Lela caught her sitting in Busha Earl's truck, she dragged her out and beat her right there. Then she shattered all the windows of the truck.

I watched from a distance, silent and afraid, as Aunt Lela paced the yard, reliving the moment. Her chest stuck out like a rooster's; she moved with confidence and fury. She believed she had every right to beat that woman. From my eavesdropping, I'd also gathered that Miss Trulie had once been involved with my father, Tutu Barrett.

Aunt Lela stomped about the yard, her rage still burning—but there was worry in her eyes, too. She knew Busha Earl would come for her.

"Busha a-go come fi mi," she told them. "Unuh cyan tell im seh mi deh yah."

And sure enough, that night, Mass Busha Earl came—and he was furious.

His voice boomed from outside the gate.

"Look yah! Weh Lela deh? She deh yah?"

Mama and I were locked inside the house with Aunt Lela and Ma Jane. I stood by the door, trembling, my heart pounding as I heard Ma Jane grunt.

Tata Joe stood at the doorway, facing Busha Earl.

"'Lela live yah?" he asked calmly.

"Man, tell har fi come out yah!" Busha Earl shouted. "Mi know she inna di house!"

But Tata Joe didn't move.

"If yuh think she in yah, come nuh... come see if she in yah."

Aunt Lela started toward the door, but Mama and Ma Jane restrained her.

"Open di door," she whispered.

But they begged her to hide beneath the bed. They knew what Busha Earl was capable of—he was a man known for hitting women.

"Miss Mary, open di door!" he bellowed, relentless.

But he eventually realized Lela wouldn't come out, and after a while, he left, still fuming.

Before that day, I couldn't recall ever seeing Aunt Lela afraid of anything or anyone.

And even after that day, I still believed she was the bravest person I knew.

Lela

BEFORE I HAD MY TWO CHILDREN, WHEN IT CAME TO FAMILY—ESPECIALLY my sisters—nothing else mattered more. Lucille, Virgie, and Vera meant everything to me, and I did all I could to protect them. They loved me for it.

Whenever they were in trouble, it was me—Lela—they called. And I always came.

Vera was always at odds with the men in her life. Anytime she sent for me, I'd drop whatever I was doing, and I already knew: a man had crossed her. It didn't matter to me whether she was right or wrong—no man was going to put his hands on my sister and get away with it.

I couldn't stand a man who thought hitting a woman made him strong.

Busha Earl tried that with me a few times. I made damn sure the idea never crossed his mind again.

I wasn't a frail or timid woman. I could stand up to any man—big or small—who thought he could mistreat me. They might've been taller, but I always found a way to look them square in the eye and hit back twice as hard.

Busha Earl kept other women behind my back, I knew that. He'd even beaten some of them—and they never lifted a finger in return.

Take that woman Trulie, for example. Big as a house. I dragged her from his truck one day and gave her a good beating.

I remembered seeing her at the dances with Flo's father, Tutu Barrett. It was almost comical—this giant of a woman dancing with the little shoemaker, his arms barely fitting around her waist, both of them moving smooth and in time with the music.

I never could understand why Vera kept going back to men who hurt her. Maybe she was hoping they'd change. Maybe she thought she needed them.

The one man I never had to fight—never had to threaten—was Tutu Barrett.

Tutu was a lover, not a beater. He had a weakness for women, yes, but he never laid a hand on one. And most of all, he loved my sister. He loved Vera. Truly.

10

MASS WILFRED
VERA

Clark's Town's main road ran north to south and was always busy, especially on workdays. From early in the morning, the whole town came alive—cars passing by, children being led to school by their parents, some walking alone or with little friends, dressed in neatly pressed uniforms.

The smell of baked bread drifted through the air. Most of the Chinese businesses made beef patties and cocoa bread fresh for the lunch crowd. The general stores were always full.

As for me, I was always busy tending to the children I nursed and raised. I was a good cook, and after working with my employers for so many years, I'd even picked up a bit of Chinese.

Flo was nearly ten. It was the summer of 1952, and though I was a young mother, most of the responsibility of raising her had fallen to Ma Jane and Tata Joe.

I loved my child—loved my family—but I must admit, my hunger for love, for finding myself a good man, often led me astray.

Ma Jane always warned me about the men I brought home.

"Dem cyan do nuttin fi yuh," she'd say.

I hated when she spoke badly of them, especially since she never hesitated to say it right to their faces.

I gave my heart too quickly, too easily—craving attention, craving affection.

I wasn't like my sister Lela. She always seemed in control. I had a temper just as fierce, and my words could cut deep, but somehow I always ended up in messes I couldn't clean up.

When a man hit me, I'd try to fight back—but I was never strong enough. I'd end up crying, running out the door, finding a way to send word to Lela. And she always came. She always rescued me.

But I was a fool. Because before long, I'd go back to the same man who had bloodied my face the day before.

All it took was an apology. A promise to love me.

A simple, "You're beautiful," and I'd give them everything.

I'd drop everything. I'd follow them anywhere.

That's why Lela and I argued so much.

I wasn't strong like her—not when it came to love.

Lela could stand up to any man. She didn't fear them, and when she hit back, she made sure they stayed down.

Clark's Town was full of bars where working men went to blow their pay. Some brought their wages home; others drank them dry. Lela had her own bar in Falmouth.

One night, the place was packed—music blasting, men loud with drink. A policeman, new to the district, made the mistake of slapping my sister.

The whole place went silent.

One man muttered, "Lawd a massi! Im dead now to raasclaat...im bax Lela!"

He was drunk, but he knew the weight of what had just happened.

I stood back, far from the crowd. No one dared get in Lela's way when she was angry.

She grabbed a bottle from the counter, smashed it, then drove the sharp edge straight into the man's head.

And just like that—it was done.

That was my sister. Ever strong. Always fearless.

Virgie, Lucille, and I all ran to Lela with our troubles. She was our tower of strength.

When Lucille couldn't take Charles's constant arguing anymore, it was Lela who made him stop.

As for me, I feared the day Lela wouldn't come for me.

Flo was nine. I had fallen for someone new. In my eyes, Wilfred was everything.

But Lela and Ma Jane saw right through him. I was too blinded by what I wanted to see what he really was.

And for love, I gave it all up. I followed Wilfred to Kingston.

It was the biggest mistake of my life.

———

———

———

Lela

I LOOK BACK ON THE DAYS WHEN I WAS YOUNG, AND I'M SO GRATEFUL I'M no longer that woman. Yahweh is in my life now. I had a short temper back then, and I couldn't stand to see my family mistreated. I took matters into my own hands more times than I can count.

It was a hot, sunny day when Ma Jane sent for me, saying I should come at once—something was wrong with Vera and Flo. I dropped everything and left immediately, fearing the worst for the child. Flo was nine years old.

Before I even reached the gate, I could hear Ma Jane quarrelling—shouting at Vera, her pet—and I wondered what my sister had done to provoke her.

Tata Joe was there too, and I noticed something strange: he was siding with Ma Jane. That was unusual. He usually stood with us, even when we were wrong. But that day, it felt like the whole yard had turned against Vera.

I didn't take sides—not until I knew what had happened.

As I stepped closer, Vera shot me a scathing look. She hadn't expected me to back her, and the look told me she assumed I wouldn't.

"Whaap'm?" I asked.

Vera pivoted, pulling Flo close to her side. I looked at my niece and saw the fear in her eyes. She was terrified.

Ma Jane had her pipe in hand and pointed it at Vera. "Lela, chat some sense inna yuh sista," she said. "Wah di hell she a-go bring di pickney guh ah Town fah?"

Vera glared back. "Ah my pickney."

"Come, Vera," Tata Joe added. "Yuh cyan bring Flo guh Town…"

Ma Jane sucked her teeth. "Imagine, she a-go carry di pickney guh live wid dat man."

I knew exactly who she meant. Wilfred.

The same Wilfred who'd given Vera a bloody lip.

Possessive Wilfred.

Jealous Wilfred.

The man who expected Vera to support him while he offered nothing but bruises and control.

I looked at my sister as I stepped closer to Flo. The child's eyes bulged, caught between us, unsure what to do.

I said, "Vera, yuh waan guh ah Town, but Flo nah guh."

Vera had already packed the bags. She'd made all the arrangements to move away with that man.

"Come, Flo!"

The child began to weep. I had gripped one of her arms, Vera the other.

We pulled.

We tugged.

Ma Jane and Tata Joe stood by, pleading with Vera to leave the child.

But my sister was as stubborn as I was strong.

Eventually, we both let go, and in the heat of the moment, Vera clawed at my face—just like she used to when we were children.

So I did what I felt was necessary. I slapped sense into my little sister.

Between Ma Jane's shouting and Tata Joe's pleading, we fought. Flo's weeping grew louder. Neighbours came out to watch from their gates.

Vera did everything to win, but I was stronger. And when she realized she couldn't overpower me, she did the unthinkable—bit into my breast with all her strength.

That was the end of the fight.

It was Ma Jane who finally gave in. I was adamant: Flo was not going to Kingston to live with an abusive, worthless man, no matter how much Vera claimed to love him.

"Mek shi gwaan!" Ma Jane snapped. Furious, she tapped ashes from her pipe and popped it into her mouth. "Shi seh ah fe har pickney...mek shi gwaan."

It was one of the rare times I'd seen disappointment in Vera spark in Ma Jane's green eyes.

She turned away, barely glancing at Flo, who was still crying.

When Tata Joe tried to comfort the child, Ma Jane told him to leave her be. If Vera suddenly knew what was best for the child, then so be it.

Ma Jane had been deeply hurt. She worried for Flo, but she was never the begging type.

She muttered one of her old sayings and that was it.

"Unuh gwaan."

She didn't say goodbye.

Flora

. . .

IT WAS SUMMER BREAK, AND I WAS PLEASED TO BE FREE OF THE DAILY school routine. But the thought of leaving home was terrifying.

We traveled to Kingston in silence. I stared out the window of the crowded bus as Clark's Town—the only world I'd ever known—drifted away behind me. I was nine years old. A part of me was excited to see the city; I'd heard others talk about Kingston with awe. But I didn't want to leave my family. I was heartbroken to leave Tata Joe and Ma Jane. I didn't know when I'd see them again.

I wasn't sure how long Mama had been planning to move to Kingston. She never mentioned it—until the day she arrived to take me away. She'd already left her job working for the Chinese families and had moved to the city weeks earlier, so I hadn't seen her in some time.

As sad as I was, there was still a small thrill inside me. Kingston was a mystery, and I was curious.

Mama had never had to spank me; I'd never given her reason to. She was playful, lenient, more like a big sister than a mother. Elegant, pretty—Mama had always felt like someone just slightly older who took care of me.

But that day, as we journeyed to Kingston, I realized something had changed. Mama wasn't my big sister anymore. She was my mother again.

Her cheekbones were bruised, her lip slightly swollen from the struggle with Aunt Lela. She didn't speak much. Only once, when we were leaving Top Town and heading toward Clark's Town's main road, did she speak—and all she said was, "Stop the crying."

I dried my tears quickly. She'd said it with such force that, for the first time in my life, I feared her.

The trip took over three hours. I knew we were close, not because Mama said anything, but because her whole demeanour changed.

She was happy again. Smiling.

And then I saw why.

Mass Wilfred was waiting for us.

He was smiling, too.

Suddenly, I was afraid again.

Flora

MASS WILFRED WAS A STRONG MAN, ALWAYS ANGRY ABOUT ONE THING OR another. He and Mama had rented a single room in Kingston where we all lived together. It wasn't far from the main road, just a few lanes away from the town square, which was always alive with buses, honking horns, and loud chatter.

Kingston was massive, but to me, it felt a lot like Clark's Town—only with better homes, less open space, and far fewer trees. Our landlord was an old woman with many tenants. There was an aging wooden kitchen and a toilet out back. Mama had even gotten a cat.

It seemed I would be in Kingston for a very long time.

Mass Wilfred hardly spoke to me. He barely acknowledged me—almost like he didn't want me there. But he knew. He knew I hated him. Knew I feared him more. I saw it in the narrow slits of his eyes.

He was tall and well-built, but he wasn't handsome. Not by a long shot. Mama was beautiful—she had the nicest figure I'd ever seen—and even at nine years old, I couldn't understand what she'd seen in a man like him.

Mama had always been a good cook, a gift she'd picked up from Ma Jane and her time working for the Chinese families. I only ever saw Mass Wilfred smile when he was eating. The rest of the time, he was a grouch—demanding, barking orders at Mama like a drill sergeant.

Still, Mama talked back. Fought back. She wasn't afraid to raise her voice, even when he raised his hands. But he was strong. Too strong. And whenever things got heated, Mama always made sure I was outside before she locked herself in the room with him.

But the walls were thin. I heard it all—the shouting, the thumps, the slaps.

By the third week of living in Kingston, I was begging Mama to go back home. Things had gotten worse. Much worse. And I could see in Mama's eyes that she wanted to leave him.

The fights had become so brutal that I feared Mama would end up dead.

One morning, when most of the tenants had already gone off to work, Mass Wilfred struck Mama so hard her lip split open.

That scar stayed with her for the rest of her life.

There was no time to get me out of the house. I pressed my back to the wall, eyes wide with horror, as he moved closer, reeking of rum, fists clenched, rage in his voice.

Mama grabbed the first thing she could find—a pair of large scissors.

"Gweh from mi!" she warned.

His fist crashed into her mouth.

"Wah yuh a-go duh?" he jeered. "Stab mi wid sizzas?"

Mama jabbed at him—missed the first time.

But something had changed. Her eyes had gone wild, filled with rage and something even deeper—something like desperation.

She didn't cry.

The second jab struck his face.

Mass Wilfred staggered back, stunned.

Mama stepped toward him, fearless now. It must've been the look in her eyes that made him bolt.

He ran.

Mama chased him.

As he reached the front gate, she threw the scissors.

I stood frozen, hand over my mouth, watching in disbelief.

The scissors missed his back by inches—one blade lodged in the gatepost, the handles still trembling.

Lela

I WAS ALWAYS A WOMAN OF PRINCIPLE. BUT IF ANYONE I CARED FOR WAS ever in need, I was willing to help. So when Vera telephoned and begged me to come to Kingston and rescue her from Wilfred, I didn't refuse.

My sister had told me long before she moved that the relationship with Wilfred wasn't good.

"Lela," Vera said over the phone, voice trembling, "duh...mi deh beg yuh! Mi cyan tek it. Lela, di man wicked! Lela, duh...cum fi mi."

I spoke with a cousin of mine, Johnny, who owned a truck. I paid him to drive to Kingston and collect my sister—along with all the furniture she'd gathered.

Vera had known what Wilfred was like, yet she'd gone back to him, bringing Flo into that situation. Just weeks earlier, she had fought me and even bitten me for trying to make her see sense. She'd left with Flo for Kingston, proud and headstrong—only to return to Clark's Town, forced to start all over again.

My eldest daughter, Pauline, was just a baby when Vera and Flo came back. At the time, I was living in Sherwood—a small town in Trelawny we simply call Sharewood. I let my sister and my niece stay in one of my spare rooms. Things were going well for me. I was thirty-two and had worked hard to accomplish my goals, especially after being turned out of the house by Ma Jane at twenty—for nothing more than going to a dance.

Shortly after Vera left with Flo, I'd gone to see Aunt P. She had always been my counsel, my confidant. Mrs. Pickersgill-Hoffstead had been a great help to me over the years. I'd never forgotten how she took me in and guided me.

I went to share my good news: the owner of the rental property where I'd been raised by Ma Jane and Tata Joe had decided to sell. I bought the property and allowed Ma Jane and the others to keep living there.

It struck me as strange—twelve years to the day after Ma Jane turned me out, I was the one who bought the very home she'd denied me.

I told Aunt P, and she only smiled and nodded.

"Leli," she said, "did I not tell you that you would be the Joseph in your family?"

I didn't understand at first. But she explained:

"Joseph was sold by his brothers," she said, "but it was through that same Joseph that they were able to leave where they were and go down to Egypt."

I gave Vera enough time to get settled before I told her she needed to find a place of her own. As I said, I'm a woman of principle. I let her and Flo stay with me when they returned from Kingston, but I hadn't forgotten how she left in the first place. She'd fought me, said terrible things—and while I forgave her, I hadn't forgotten.

Vera went to Ma Jane to complain that I was putting her out. Soon after, Ma Jane showed up, furious.

"She haffi stay deh," she said. "Weh yuh expect har fi guh?"

Granny insisted I let Vera move back into the house we'd grown up in—the house I now owned. But I wouldn't hear of it. I'd already done more than enough.

That day, I gave my entire family notice to leave my land.

When Vera came to beg me to change my mind, I simply said, "Shi nuh business fi tell mi suh."

I wasn't pleased that Ma Jane was trying to dictate terms. After everything Vera had said and done, Granny still wanted to act like nothing happened—like we could just go back to how things were.

But I couldn't.

It was hard, but I hardened my heart and stood my ground.

A few days later, a neighbour came to see me—a man we called Postie, because he delivered the mail in Clark's Town. He was one of the kindest men we knew, and probably the only person who could have convinced Ma Jane and Vera to make peace.

Postie was tall and wiry, with a happy grin that always exposed the absence of most of his teeth. Nearly everyone in Top Town had heard about the fight between Vera and me—the day she took Flo to live with that worthless man.

But Granny was never one to admit she was wrong. Vera was the same.

Postie paid them a visit and told them they'd handled things all wrong. It was his intervention that brought the solution. He encouraged them to apologize, and to my surprise, they did.

I accepted the apology.

And I let them continue living on the property.

11

BYE BYE WILFRED
LELA

After Vera reluctantly left him, Wilfred had moved on, making certain Vera knew he'd found himself a new woman. I had forgotten all about Wilfred, for it appeared Vera had happily moved on.

I left Sherwood early one morning—I wanted to visit with my family. Upon arriving at Vera's, I found Ma Jane and Tata Joe going about their business, while Vera was busy cooking. Cooking and dressing up had always made my sister happy; she relied heavily on her beauty and domestic skills to please her lovers. It was probably how she tried to keep them. But what Vera had not learned over the years was that a man needed to love her for the person she was. Vera was a good woman, yet she hardly knew it—or even believed it.

Flo was there too, always polite, but I could never understand why the child always seemed afraid when in my presence. Maybe she saw something in me that reminded her of Wilfred—or worse, of what I was capable of.

I walked into the house, surprised to find that Vera's bed was gone.

"Weh yuh bed?" I asked.

Vera pivoted nervously, unwilling to meet my eyes. Flo had gone to sit with Ma Jane on the other side of the property, where she roomed with Tata Joe.

Vera said, "Mi bed dung ah Granny."

I looked at my sister, perplexed. Why would her bed be at the old woman's house—a woman to whom we had no relation? Everyone called her Granny, this old woman who lived nearby.

"Why?" I asked.

Vera stuttered, still pivoting and hooking her forefingers together. "Wilfred... Wilfred seh him deh cum fi di bed."

I said, "Guh back fi it." I was already heading for the door. "Guh back fi de bed. Put back di bed inna di house... anytime Wilfred cum fi it, send cum call mi."

Several days later, early in the evening, Flo came running to my house in tears.

"Mass Wilfred cum fi de bed!" she said.

My second child, Claudia, was just a newborn babe, and I dropped her hard into the crib. If that mattress had not been a good one, my child would have probably had a broken back, for I literally dropped her.

I arrived at the house with Flo to find Wilfred cursing, raising his voice, and making a fuss about wanting his bed back. Ma Jane and Tata Joe were bold, but they were also much older and could've done nothing to keep that man from entering the house.

I didn't hit Wilfred. I simply held him—hard—so the wretch couldn't run. Furious, I commanded Vera to get a piece of wood. As I held Wilfred down, I told her to beat the brute with it. And my sister did. She hit him with all her might, for she saw the rage in my eyes. One of Vera's blows caught me in the head, but I still held Wilfred down.

After I felt Vera had beaten him enough, I let go, and together we walked to the police station. I had devised the perfect plan to be rid of him.

I am a changed woman now, but when I arrived at that station, I told all manner of lies—all the terrible things Wilfred said he would come back and do to us. And maybe he would have. But I wasn't going to wait to find out.

The police believed my lies and ordered Wilfred never to return to the area again.

Wilfred was finally out of Vera's life.

Flora

MASS WILFRED WAS FINALLY OUT OF MAMA'S LIFE. HOWEVER, I CANNOT say she was happy about it, for she'd loved him. Mama spent weeks—months, even—pining over the man who had told her he no longer wanted her, who claimed to have found himself another woman.

Eventually, Mama moved on from her sorrows. As her former employers—the Chinese families—had adored her so, she was quickly back in their employ shortly after we returned from Kingston. They welcomed her with a small celebration at their home, as if no time had passed.

Much had changed over the years. By the time I was fifteen, Ma Jane —my great-grandmother, the woman who had raised three generations —was eighty-nine. During my childhood, back when I attended Clark's Town Primary School, I'd become friends with Gloria Allen. Gloria was nicknamed Pet. I'd spent many days at the Allen household in Bottom Town, and Pet often visited my home at Top Town. We were inseparable.

My other close friend, however, was a girl Mama never approved of.

"Lef dat gal company," Mama told me more than once.

But I didn't listen. I kept my friendship with Doreen. And after

Mama discovered I'd defied her, I believe that was the only time she ever laid her hands on me. I could never understand why Mama disliked my friend so much. Maybe she saw something in Doreen that I couldn't see.

By the time I was nearly sixteen, Mama had left the choosing of my friends up to me. I remained friends with Doreen.

Mama and I lived in one section of the house at Top Town, while Ma Jane and Tata Joe lived in the other. Each room had its own entrance. Tata Joe, meanwhile, had been carrying on his own quiet rivalry with two other men his age—one Buttie MacFarlane, known as Buttie Mac, and Baboo Slowly. I cannot say why these two men despised Tata Joe, or why he disliked them so. They were old, and I was too young to understand—or care.

Still, those men hardly ever had anything nice to say about Ma Jane's husband.

My grandmother, Bernice Bolt—Granny B, as we all called her—had begun to fall ill. She was slowly losing her eyesight. My aunts—Lucille, Virgie, and Lela—visited her often, as she still resided in Falmouth.

Aunt Lela had also given permission for a small church to be built at one end of the property. Our place of dwelling had now become a place of worship for the Church of Yahweh. Once a week, I heard the singing and the teachings. The Yahweh church sang with their guitars and accordions; they clapped their hands and raised their voices aloud in songs and praises. Their music stirred the air like a blessing or a warning—I was never sure which.

Mama had found happiness again. She'd fallen in love once more. And when Mama was in love, nothing else seemed to matter.

———

12

SUN 'BROWN' VIRGO
VERA

I was not yet forty when a new man came into my life. Others called him Sun Brown—or Sun Virgo, for his surname was Virgo. I simply called him Sun, or by his first name, Vincent. And I loved him dearly.

Flo and I still lived in the house where we'd both been raised by Ma Jane, and we were happy there. My daughter was nearly sixteen, already a young woman. Except for her friendship with that Doreen, I'd never had any problems with my child. Not only was Flo beautiful, but she was also a well-mannered young lady—stubborn in her own way, yes—but we were close. More like sisters, really. It was Ma Jane who had mothered us both.

Sun was from Duncans, a carpenter by trade. He was tall and dark, with a muscular build. Our relationship flourished quickly, and for the first time in my life, I felt I had found the man I would marry—a man I could truly call my own, one I wouldn't have to share with another woman. Somehow, I felt Sun was different.

However, Ma Jane and Lela never liked him.

Ma Jane's opinion was that I needed a man who would change my life—someone who could provide for me. But Granny never really understood. Being a carpenter wasn't easy. Business slowed sometimes, and money got tight.

So, I did what I believed a good woman should do: I tried my best to help him...to make things easier.

And deep down, I believed Sun was the man I would be with forever.

Flora

OTHERS MAY HAVE CALLED MAMA'S NEW GENTLEMAN FRIEND SUN Brown. I didn't like that name—or him, for that matter. His true name was Vincent Virgo. I hardly ever spoke to the man, but whenever I had to address him, it was either Mr. Virgo or simply Sun. Mama wanted me to like him, but I saw nothing special about this one—nothing to set him apart from the rest of the men she'd brought into our lives.

I learned early on never to make the same mistakes Mama had where men were concerned. If a man couldn't love and respect me, he didn't deserve me. Mama never seemed to understand that. She loved with her whole heart—loved them more than she loved herself, it seemed.

With separate entrances, the two rooms of our small house had become two households: one side held Mama and me, the other, Ma Jane and Tata Joe. I was still a teenager, not yet eighteen, but I knew the signs. When Mama was in the best of moods for several days, there was always a new man. One could tell. She took more care getting dressed —not that she ever let herself go; Mama was always immaculate. But when there was a man around, she became different—more playful, almost childlike. She went to great lengths to make him happy: gifts, well-cooked meals, attention fit for a king. Sun's visits grew more frequent until eventually, he moved in.

Mama never discussed it with me. One evening, as I was inside reading, he arrived—with his belongings in hand and nothing said. Mama stood there, shifting from side to side, fingers laced in front of her like a schoolgirl about to be scolded.

I asked one simple question.

"Mama, weh him a-go sleep?"

She kept pivoting, avoiding my eyes, before answering softly,

"Inna di bed."

I looked toward the one bed we shared.

"Mi nah stay in yah wid him," I said. I walked past Sun, not sparing him a second glance, and crossed over to Ma Jane's side of the house.

Over the next few months, Sun enjoyed every kindness Mama could offer. She did everything to make him comfortable. There was talk all over Clark's Town—how Vera had taken Sun in and made something of him. She bought him new clothes and shoes, fed him well, and made sure he was trimmed each week at the barbershop. People said she'd found the man of her dreams, the one who would finally make her his wife.

But they didn't see what I saw.

They argued constantly.

Sun was no different from the others—just as possessive, just as abusive, just as violent. Still, each day, Mama made sure his clothes were clean. She made sure he came home to a tidy house and a table set with polished cutlery and a hot, delicious meal—things he clearly never had before her. It was expected that he would marry the woman who'd lifted him up in life.

Ma Jane didn't care for Sun, but she tolerated him. I remember one day when he stepped out into the yard wearing a crisp new outfit Mama had bought. Ma Jane looked at Tata Joe and me, grunted, and said,

"What a way fi him marina white…"

I chuckled to myself. Mama had made sure Sun had the best—while she got his worst.

Their relationship was turbulent. Sometimes, after a bad argument, he would pack his things and leave. Once, he struck her and moved out. I thought it was finally over, so I moved back in with Mama. We resumed sharing the one bed.

Then one night, all was still. The only sounds were insects chirping in the dark and the distant barking of mongrels. I heard the creak of the door but thought nothing of it. Slowly, I came fully awake—and saw him.

There, in the corner of the room, sat a bulky figure in the dark. I could make out the whites of Sun's eyes, staring at Mama and me as we lay in the bed.

I sprang up and ran. I was in my nightie. I left the room and crossed back over to Ma Jane's side of the house.

Mama may have been angry.

But I didn't care.

Vera

SUN AND I MAY NOT HAVE HAD THE PERFECT RELATIONSHIP, BUT I LOVED him. We had our differences, sure, but I believed—truly believed—that he would marry me. I was good to him. Every relationship had its hard times, and mine with Sun was no different from any other couple's, as far as I saw it.

Flo had met a young man, Goskel Johnson—a policeman. I never liked the boy from the start. Something in his eyes, the way he smiled...

he struck me as a gal man. But he had a good job, and I thought maybe he could make my child happy. I warned Flo about him, told her to be careful. Still, when she came and told me she was moving to Kingston with Mr. Johnson, I gave them my blessing. The boy even came to me himself to ask permission.

But when I found out he was mistreating my child, I got on the first bus to Kingston. I told Goskel Johnson straight—I didn't raise Flo for that kind of treatment, and I wouldn't sit by and let him harm her. I brought my daughter back to Clark's Town myself.

The relationship didn't end there. It continued, and by August of 1960—shortly after Flo's seventeenth birthday—she was pregnant. Every time that man came around, I looked at him and thought I could kill him. And that girl, Doreen—the friend I'd warned Flo about? She'd bring nothing but trouble into our lives...

13

BROKEN FRIENDSHIPS

FLORA

I was lucky enough to be employed at Clark's Town's post office, but once word got out that I was with child, people started talking. Everyone wanted to know how Miss Vera's daughter, Flo, had gotten pregnant and still managed to keep her job. That position was coveted by many young women. But I didn't lose my job. I worked right up to my ninth month.

My life had changed drastically in just a year. When I met Goskel Johnson, I never imagined I'd one day have his child. I remember the first time I saw him—standing outside a shop near the police cruiser. He was dark and tall, handsome, in his uniform. I had stayed in school longer than most girls my age, and as I walked home that afternoon, he called out to me. At first, I ignored him. Then I heard the sound of his quick footsteps catching up behind me.

"Pretty girl... young Miss..." he said.

Days after that first meeting, Doreen and I spent hours giggling about him. She brought me the first message from Goskel and encouraged me to meet him. He wanted her to formally introduce us —and she did, just like he asked. By the time I became pregnant, I believed there wasn't another man on God's earth I could love the way I loved that policeman. I was sure I would become his wife. And all the while, Doreen kept pushing me toward him, reminding me how lucky I was.

But in my fourth month, something changed. Doreen started avoiding me. Her mother and grandmother, once kind to me, barely acknowledged my presence. They just looked at my swelling belly with cold eyes. I didn't understand it. Doreen and I had been inseparable. There'd been no argument, no falling out—just silence.

When I brought it up to Goskel, he laughed. That same low, sly chuckle he always had.

"Heh, heh, heh... ah jealous shi jealous... heh heh..."

He smiled, his eyes glittering. And I believed him.

Then even Lola and Nester, two other close friends, turned their backs on me. They walked past me in the streets like I was a stranger. I let them go. I wasn't one to beg people to be my friend. I told myself again—Doreen was just jealous.

One evening, when Mama's man, Sun Virgo, was out, Mama, Ma Jane, and I sat down for a talk. Well, more of a lecture. It was Ma Jane who brought it up first.

"Di gyal deh," she said. "Yuh nuh si shi deh breed."

I looked at Mama. They'd clearly discussed this already.

Mama pointed a finger at me. "Mi tell yuh from long time fi leff dat gal company... but yuh nuh listen. Look weh yuh end up now!"

"What, Mama? Doreen? Wah yuh deh talk bout?"

Mama let out a deep sigh and shook her head.

"Whappen, Mama?"

Ma Jane held her pipe between her lips, smoke curling out her nose. She took a long breath, her frail chest rising and falling.

"Gyal pickney, open yuh yai!" she said, her voice raspy but firm. "Di police bwoy breed di two ah unuh!"

I froze. My heart pounded. In that moment, everything made sense. Doreen's silence. Her mother's scorn. The way her granny's lip curled when she passed me on the street. It was true. I knew it was.

Goskel confirmed it later, though he tried to twist it. When I confronted him, he smiled in that same smug way, dressed in his uniform like nothing was wrong.

"Flo, yuh nuh see wah shi deh duh? Shi ah ginnal. Shi gimmi jacket," he said.

By claiming she'd named him the father of another man's child, he'd confessed everything. He'd lain with Doreen—the girl I thought was my best friend. And now, we were both carrying the same man's child. Doreen was due in April, and I was due in May of 1961.

14

CURSE OF THE JANCRO

FLORA

Doreen and my other friends had all turned against me as soon as they learned I was with child. The fool I was hadn't realized that all along, Doreen had wanted Goskel Johnson for herself—and she'd had him, for we'd both become pregnant at the same time. I shuddered at the thought of it—my best friend deceiving me in such a way.

My friend Pet stood by me through it all. Her father, Pastor Nathaniel Allen—known to everyone as Bredda Nattie—was a good, wise little man. Bredda Nattie was the founder and spiritual leader of one of the revival churches in Bottom Town. While Ma Jane rarely attended church, she often went to Bredda Nattie's street meetings, and Mama, too, sometimes visited his services.

I referred to Pastor Allen as a *"little man"* only because was small in stature. I smile when I think of him. As Pet and I became like sisters, so did her father become a father figure to me. Over the years, Pet and I had built a strong, inseparable bond.

My relationship with my child's father continued, but I barely saw Goskel anymore—he'd been transferred to Kingston. I was distraught. The man had deceived me. For the first time, I understood what Mama must have felt—why she'd clung to a man who brought nothing but pain. But I knew I had to be stronger than that.

I learned a hard lesson in those months. I told myself it was folly to have a child for a policeman. To have a policeman for a spouse was the worst thing a woman could do—it seemed they had a woman or two in every parish. Goskel came back to Clark's Town only every few months. For me, carrying his child, that was not enough. He insisted Doreen was lying about her pregnancy, but I never believed him. He paid her little attention, which only made Doreen more bitter—and it infuriated her mother and grandmother, who were hoping Goskel would choose her over me.

As the weeks passed, I thought about life before Goskel. I wondered if I would have met him at all, had another path opened. There had been another young man who once showed interest in me. I liked him very much. Everyone called him Keith Longmore, though that wasn't his real name. Keith was a nickname; Longmore was the surname of his foster parents. His real name was Carl McEwan.

But life has a strange way of deciding things. Just as I was beginning to know him, Keith went away. His grandmother had decided to return to Jamaica after many years in Bermuda, and with her, he left Clark's Town. I lost touch with the friend I once traded comics with.

As my pregnancy progressed, Mama and Sun grew close again, and he moved back in. I decided to move back to Ma Jane's side of the house, where I had my own spot in the bed, just against the wall. Tata Joe slept on a smaller bed in the same room. At night, Ma Jane and I would lie awake and talk for hours. Tata Joe would tell jokes—funny ones that had me laughing so hard, I worried I might deliver the baby then and there.

It took Ma Jane a little longer to loosen up and laugh, but soon she did. Even Mama, from the other side of the house, was laughing, while Sun grumbled that it was too late.

"Wah unu deh laugh 'bout?" I heard him suck his teeth. "Yuh a eediat? Vera, gwaan guh sleep!"

But Mama's laughter was always contagious, and that night, though a wooden wall separated us, we heard her screeching with laughter.

Tears ran down her face, and one last joke from Tata Joe—a good one —was enough to infect even the grouchy Sun Virgo, who finally joined in. He, too, laughed uncontrollably.

———

———

———

Vera

MY CHILDBEARING YEARS WERE LONG BEHIND ME. AFTER HAVING FLO, I was never able to conceive again. Later, I had to get a hysterectomy, and I came to terms with the fact that I was meant to have just one child— for I had lost two before Flo came into this world.

Sun had come home again, and since his return, we had hardly exchanged a cross word. One night, after we'd all laughed at Tata Joe's jokes, Sun pulled me close to him in bed. He whispered in my ear that he loved me—and in that moment, I knew I would be his wife. It was only a matter of time before we would marry.

That night, the warmth of his breath against my neck, the softness of his lips as he covered mine, set my body afire. Sun had never been good with words. He was jealous, quick to anger—but he knew how to love me. He appreciated the woman I was. Wrapped in his arms, I felt I belonged to him, and I longed to become his wife. I also knew I could never give him a child. Yet my body welcomed his with a boundless passion—for he was mine, and I was his.

I was at work one day at Oswald Chin's shop when I heard a commotion out on the main road. I stepped outside to see what had stirred the town. To my surprise, what I saw was a big jancro.

A vulture.

No one dared touch it. Jancros were terrible scavengers, and everyone knew they circled above before or after death. Many times I'd seen Ma Jane look up at those black creatures, pull her pipe from her lips, and grunt, "Somebody going dead." And sure enough, before the end of the day, news would come that someone had passed—sometimes that very morning, sometimes the night before.

But this one wasn't flying. It walked slowly along the road, unbothered by the crowd gathering around it. That alone chilled my bones. A jancro walking? Never before had I seen such a thing. These birds lived in the sky, not on our streets.

Some said it must've had a broken wing. But the creature looked strong—proud, even. It cocked its bald head and paced like it was searching for something. Still, no one got too close.

Then one fool by the road started singing:

> *Dis long time gal mi neva see you*
> *Come let mi hole yuh han.*
> *Peel head Jancro sit pan the tree top*
> *Pick out the blossom*
> *Let mi hole yuh han Gal*
> *Let mi hole yuh han...*

> *Dis long time gal mi neva see you*
> *Come let mi wheel an' tun*
> *Dis long time gal mi neva see you*
> *Come let mi wheel an' tun.*
> *Peel head Jancro sit pan the tree top*
> *Pick out the blossom*
> *Let mi wheel an' tun gal,*
> *Let mi wheel an' tun...*

AND SOON ENOUGH, ALL THE FOOLS—MOSTLY MEN—JOINED IN, SINGING the old folk song loud and gleeful as if they didn't know better.

But I knew better. I am a superstitious woman, and deep in my belly, I knew that was no good sign.

Jancros visited the dead—not the living.

To see one walking the streets of Clark's Town was a terrible thing.

———————

———————

———————

Flora

I WAS NEARLY IN MY SEVENTH MONTH OF PREGNANCY, AND IT HAD BEEN one of the hottest days in Jamaica. I was hot, restless, and had been home with my grandparents, having reduced my work hours at the post office. I sat beneath the orange tree, seeking shade from the harsh sun. In the distance, I watched the haze shimmer, and the heat made me dizzy. Despite the heat, I found some comfort in the breeze and the songs of the birds. It was an extremely humid day, but I was grateful for the shade.

Tata Joe was at the far end of the yard tending to the pigs, and Ma Jane sat on the steps outside the tiny wooden kitchen shack, her back against the doorframe, pipe in her mouth. She was nodding off into slumber. Granny B, Mama's mother, had moved back to Clark's Town with us. Since Mama and Sun were once again in the midst of a separation, Granny B shared the second room of the house with her.

The day passed quickly, and as the sun began to disappear beyond the horizon, the island slowly cooled. Nightfall came, and I was just about ready for bed when I heard Ma Jane mutter a curse.

To my astonishment, I saw what caused her to speak that way—a big black jancro, walking through the yard. It hopped up the three steps and entered the house. "Tata Joe!" Ma Jane called, as she moved quickly despite her age, leaning against her cane.

I was frozen in place, shock flooding my senses. Ma Jane, too, seemed shaken, though she moved swiftly, her fear hidden behind her usual demeanour. "Wah di hell dis jancro ah du out a night?" she muttered. We all watched as the jancro calmly walked into the house. Tata Joe followed it inside, but Ma Jane stayed close behind, her green eyes filled with apprehension.

"Tan weh yuh deh, Flo! Nuh move!" she ordered, but I couldn't obey. I had to see why a jancro—of all things—had walked through the yard and gone into the house. I stood at the door, my heart pounding in my chest.

What I saw next stunned me to my core. The jancro, with its bald pink head and sleek black feathers, jumped onto the bed I shared with Ma Jane and settled in my spot as if it meant to nest there. The creature lay still, staring blankly, as if waiting. It didn't move or react to the presence of Tata Joe or Ma Jane.

I could not go any closer. Ma Jane's voice was firm, "Dem send di jancro fi cum kill yuh pickney...and kill yuh..."

By the time Mama and Granny B arrived from the other side of the house, Mr. Brady, our neighbour, had come over. He had heard the commotion and wanted to see what was happening. He told us that he had seen the jancro walking toward the house earlier that day and wondered if it was sick. Ma Jane, puzzled and suspicious, grunted.

The jancro had walked all the way from the main road, up the lane to Top Town, and directly into my bed. Many people in Clark's Town had seen it walking in the hot sun, paying no mind to anyone around it. It was the behaviour of this creature that had everyone uneasy.

Mama was the first to voice what others were thinking. "Beanie an har muma try kill mi pickney," she said. "Dem wuk obeah pon yuh!" She was talking about Doreen and her family—suggesting they were using witchcraft to harm me and my child.

Fear gripped me. I wanted nothing more than to leave the yard, to escape from the suffocating air and the weight of all the superstition surrounding me. But Granny B stopped me when I tried to leave. "Stay in di yard, Flo," she warned. "Don't go walkin' out deh."

I was angry. I wanted to run, to get away from the fear and the strange happenings around me, but they wouldn't let me. The night was unbearable.

We hardly slept that night. After Tata Joe struck the jancro with his walking stick, he took it outside and burned it by the Calabash Tree. I was terrified. The creature didn't struggle, nor did it make a sound as it was set ablaze. It simply accepted its fate and died quietly.

The next morning, we went to the Calabash Tree to check for the remains of the jancro, but there was nothing—not even its bones. To make matters worse, Tata Joe's arm had swollen terribly. He fell ill and was hospitalized for several days.

Mama and Ma Jane insisted that I leave the house. They believed that Doreen's family had sent the jancro to kill me and my unborn child. So, I moved to Falmouth, staying with my close friend Alcie for the remainder of my pregnancy. I only visited Clark's Town briefly to see my family.

Doreen's friends, Nester and Lola, would taunt me whenever I passed by their house. Nester would call out, "Tell mi how yuh feel when yuh cum outta wildaness!" And not long after, Lola would join in, singing the same words in mocking rhythm. "Yeh...tell mi how yuh feel wen yuh cum outa wildaness!" They would laugh, knowing full well that after the jancro had been found in my bed, I had been sent away, hidden for fear that both I and my child were in danger.

15

TATA JOE
VERA

The incident with the jancro was horrifying. I had seen the thing walking past Oswald Chin's shop, unaware it was destined for my house—sent to harm my child and grand-child. Both Ma Jane and I were convinced this was the work of that girl's mother and granny. They wanted their Doreen to have a man who never even wanted her.

As for Flo, who continued to see that policeman Johnson, she was terrified by what had happened—but also deeply in love with him.

Ma Jane believed the thing with the jancro was unnatural. Even Tata Joe, who burned that vile creature in the yard, believed it was something that girl's family had done. They wanted death.

But my sister Lela had no time for such superstitions. She wouldn't accept the truth—that the young woman's family had gone to lengths to get my child out of their way. Lucile and Virgie both agreed that Flo had to leave Clark's Town, at least for a while, or until she had the baby.

Our Tata Joe never recovered after he killed the jancro. He became sick the next morning. But despite everything, Tata Joe, humorous at heart, went on his own terms. Every time we visited him in the hospital, he told old jokes and laughed like he wasn't sick at all. The man acted as though he were just on holiday. We'd always leave the hospital laughing, convinced he'd be back home in no time.

And he did return home—but not the same as before. He had grown weak and was always falling ill in the weeks and months that followed.

One evening, after hearing that Tata Joe had gotten worse and been hospitalized again, I went to see him immediately after work. But I arrived too late. The security guard—an unfeeling swine—refused to let us in, saying visiting hours were over. Lela was with me, and not even her threats or loud mouth could get us through those doors.

The following morning, when we got word that Tata Joe had died in the night, I wept. We had been right there, and still, we weren't allowed to see him one last time. He died without a final goodbye.

Later that morning, when I returned to the hospital, the staff spoke of how funny he had been the night before. They said he had them laughing right up to his last breath. I smiled through tears. That was our Tata Joe—the man who once carried me on his back all the way from Hyde Hall to Falmouth just to see my mama.

Now he was gone. And I knew in my heart he had sacrificed himself for my child and grandchild. I didn't care what anyone else believed—whatever had come into our house that night had been sent to harm my only child, and Tata Joe had taken its wrath upon himself.

At the time of his death, Lela had already moved to Falmouth, so the hospital was close to where she lived. I returned the next morning before work to arrange for the release of the body. In those days, we kept our dead at home, packed in ice until the burial.

But when I walked into the room, I found the two men Tata Joe had disliked most—the ones he'd always been in conflict with. Baboo Slowly and Buttie Mac stood over his dead body. They were shocked to see me. One of them—that monster Buttie Mac—had a sharp knife in his hand. I screamed. There was blood on his hands, and Tata Joe's genitals were exposed.

Those superstitious, wicked fools had come to castrate him in death—to plant him, as they called it. They believed that if you castrated the dead, especially someone you had conflict with, their spirit could never return to haunt you.

That's what they were doing to my Tata Joe.

I refused to leave and sent for Lela. Buttie Mac—who was originally from St. Ann—was reluctant to leave. It wasn't until Lela and Virgie arrived that the two men finally left, disappointed that I had interrupted their vile task.

Lela threatened to call the police. Even Virgie, who was normally so passive, could barely hold her tongue. She stood firm in front of those two monsters.

"Him is not a pig!" she said. "What you deh castrate him for?"

And so Baboo Slowly and Buttie Mac left, their wicked task unfinished.

———————

———————

Flora

LOSING TATA JOE SO SUDDENLY WAS DEVASTATING, FOR HE HAD TAKEN ON the role of both father and grandfather throughout my life. The strong, tall man who had come to Clark's Town from Manchester long before I —or even Mama—was born, was gone.

Tata Joe had leased a small piece of land at Walk-a-piece—what they called the place where farmers owned or rented land for growing crops. He would go to Walk-a-piece, till the ground, and plant produce. He even built a little hut there. I remember those days clearly, when Tata Joe would take me along. He let me ride atop the donkey, all the way from home, beneath the hot sun, to the place where he grew potatoes, yam, and many other crops.

After a long day in the field, Tata Joe would always return home and take his bath right there in the yard. Ma Jane used to scold him for not bathing inside—said all of Top Town would see his nakedness—but Tata Joe didn't care.

At night, when the world turned black as pitch and fear crept in, Tata Joe would tell ghost stories by the flicker of a kerosene lamp. I was just a child, huddled in Mama's arms, eyes wide and heart racing as he spoke of the *rolling calf* and the *three-foot jack*.

My relationship with my child's father ended—he was hardly ever around after being transferred to Kingston. Doreen gave birth in April, and I in May. Mama was there when I delivered, but her superstitions got the better of her. She refused to enter the room, convinced that Doreen's mother, the granny, wanted me and my baby dead.

Still, on May 8, 1961, I gave birth to my first child, Junior Anthony Johnson, at home. The midwife, a kind woman known as Nurse Campbell, arrived just in time. One moment I was gripped by pain, and the next, he was in the world.

That child—my son—instantly became the pride and joy of our family. Small as he was, he became the third of three boys left in a household full of women—Aunt Virgie had two sons.

We called my son Bill, and Mama loved him more than anything in the world.

When I brought Bill home, Tata Joe—so frail, so ill—asked if he could hold him. I was afraid he might drop the baby, but gently, I placed Bill in his arms. He looked down at my son and smiled with such joy that day.

He died several weeks later, on May 31, 1961.

—————

—————

—————

Vera

OUR HOME WAS NEVER THE SAME AFTER TATA JOE DIED. BUT OUR FAMILY had grown.

Virgie had two sons—Boysie and his brother Hertis, whom everyone called Benny—as well as a daughter, Merle. Lela had two daughters, Pauline and Claudia. And I had Flo. So, the three boys in our family were Virgie's sons, Boysie and Benny, and Flo's baby, Bill.

By 1962, Ma Jane was ninety-three years old and began suffering from more severe chest pains. My granny was still as stern as ever, and I remained her little pet—even though I, too, had become a grand-mother. Mama—whom everyone called Granny B—had moved back to Clark's Town, having lost much of her eyesight. She could only see shadows now. My mother and grandmother were both in my care. My sisters and I did our best to look after them.

Lucille and her man, Charles, had built a life of their own, and so had Virgie. Lela worked hard and had a family of her own. Flo, a single mother, cared for her child alone, as the father was hardly ever around. Mr. Johnson came to see the child now and then, but never often enough. I saw the pain it brought Flo each time the policeman visited and then left again.

I had moved elsewhere with Sun, since the house had become overcrowded after Mama moved back to Clark's Town. Ma Jane's sister, Zit—who was deaf—had also come to live in my childhood home. Flo and her cousins simply called her Auntie.

Aunt Zit was a sad woman, always murmuring to herself. She had been childless, though she once had twins who died suddenly after birth. I often looked at her and thought I could have suffered such a fate, for I had lost two babies before having Flo. I couldn't blame Auntie for talking to herself—her life had been hard. The man she was meant to marry had left her practically waiting at the altar. She'd made her own dress, stored all her wedding things in a large tin box. He had promised to marry her. But he never did, and Auntie's heart was broken.

Flora

MAMA AND LITTLE BILL HAD GROWN VERY CLOSE. BY THE TIME MY SON was walking and starting to utter his first few words, he had become her pride and joy. The entire family adored the little man. But Mama couldn't help noticing how much he resembled his father. "Bwoy," she would say, "Johnson jus' spit him out..."

I was still working at the Clark's Town post office and would see my former friend Doreen from time to time. Neither of us exchanged a word. Her child, Barry—just a month older than Bill—had received no support at all from his father. Goskel had apparently moved on with his life, though he still visited my son whenever it suited him.

Much had changed over the months. One day I was shocked to see my old friend Carl McEwan—better known as Keith Longmore—back in Clark's Town. He had returned after caring for his grandmother in Kingston and was now working at the Clark's Town Bakery. When he walked into the post office that day, I was surprised—and somewhat excited—to see him again. I could see it in his eyes: Keith was shocked to see me with a baby.

He mentioned that his stay in Clark's Town would be short, as he planned to move to England. I was devastated to hear he intended to marry a girl abroad. One evening, he explained the whole story—he spoke of a mulatto girl whose parents had disapproved of him. She had written to him, saying she was old enough to make her own decisions and wanted to send for him to join her in England. But before those two weeks were over, Keith told me he wanted to start a life with me. Though some of my friends disapproved—insisting he was a stranger I knew nothing about—I followed my heart. Keith cancelled his plans to leave for England.

As our friendship resumed over the months, I told him everything —what had happened between Goskel and me, even the rift with Doreen. A mutual friend, Winsome, had encouraged me to give Keith a chance. Before long, we grew closer. But as our courtship deepened, the gossips stirred. Many claimed I had no intention of staying with Keith—that I only wanted the few dollars he earned at the bakery. But Keith was the best of men. He saw who I truly was and ignored the rumours. Although Mama was wary at first, he was good to both me and my child. I'll never forget one of the first gifts he gave me: a pair of sandals.

When Keith visited me at home, Ma Jane and Granny B were pleased to see him. But Zit—my great-aunt, whom everyone called Auntie—could hardly stand the sight of him.

"Mi nuh know weh Flora get dis man," she'd mutter. Auntie was a stubborn woman, her heart filled with a deep anger toward men.

Almost every evening after Keith left, Auntie would pull her large tin box from beneath the bed and call for me and my cousin Merle.

"Uno come," she'd say. "Come, Flora... come, Merlie! Yuh see all di sinting dem di man mek mi buy?"

She would open the tin box and carefully unfold the wedding gown she'd sewn with her own hands. There were always tears in her eyes as she touched the wedding items she had prepared for the man who never showed. Merle and I saw the pain in her eyes—her dainty hands trembling as she refolded the white dress and placed it atop the wedding shoes, hose, and all the other adornments. In Auntie, we saw not just sorrow, but a darkness that seemed to live within her, a shadow left by the man who had once promised her a future. She often spoke to herself and became angry over the smallest things—even if Merle and I politely declined food she had cooked. So full or not, we never refused what she offered. We stuffed ourselves and listened as she reminded us that men could never be trusted.

One day, after another of Auntie's complaints, I finally asked Keith what was going on. She had said he was a rude man with no manners. As it turned out, the entire issue was a simple misunderstanding.

Auntie was deaf. Keith would visit, and she claimed he never greeted her, which only added to her resentment. But Keith was confused.

"Flo, listen to me," he said. "Every time mi come deh, mi seh, 'Evening, Miss Zit.' She never answer, so mi stop seh it."

Keith shrugged, his brows knitted together. He hated when people passed judgment on us or questioned his intentions. He was a proud man who didn't like others telling him who he should love or what choices to make.

"Keith, Auntie deaf," I said at last, realizing I had never told him.

We laughed about it that evening. All along, Auntie thought Keith was a brute with no manners, while he thought she was ignoring him out of spite. In truth, they simply hadn't heard—or understood—each other. After that, Keith made sure to greet Auntie in ways she could see. She nodded at him with a faint grin. But even so, after every visit, Merle and I noticed that Auntie would pull out her old tin box again. She would touch the dress, the shoes, the veil. It was as if she had to remind herself that men were cruel, no matter how kind they seemed.

16

SUN VIRGO'S BRIDE
VERA

My relationship with Sun deteriorated quickly, though I had always believed he was the man for me. Like most of the other men in my past, Sun was ten years my junior. That was just the way it turned out—or maybe just how I preferred things to be. I never doubted that one day I'd become Mrs. Vincent Virgo. Strange, how much I loved him—he reminded me, in a way I hated to admit, of that fool who caused me to lose my first child. Many nights I lay awake thinking of that pain, the hollow feeling of pushing a lifeless baby into the world. I despised that man and his awful grin. But Sun was different—or so I told myself. It was a pity I couldn't give him a child.

Flo had been in her ninth month of pregnancy when Sun and I had our worst quarrel. In the heat of the moment, in his rage, he struck me in the house. And I, vengeful and sometimes hot-tempered, struck him back. At the time, we weren't living together—our relationship had always been a rocky one. Sun was a jealous man, easily angered if another man so much as looked at me. He came close, spitting hateful words in my face, his breath warm and sour. I wouldn't back down, and neither would he. It was Flo, belly swollen with her unborn child, who forced herself between us, using every ounce of strength she had to pry us apart.

Later that evening, the policeman—Flo's child's father—showed up. He had heard about the incident and told Sun plainly that if he ever came back to the house, he'd put him in jail. Goskel Johnson meant every word.

Though our relationship continued after that, Sun and I lived apart. After Flo gave birth, I watched her relationship with the policeman slowly unravel. She had always been a strong girl—stronger than I had ever been in matters of love. When Keith returned to Clark's Town, it took time before he and Flo began courting, but soon there was talk. I never quite trusted the man they called Keith Longmore—though he was handsome and admired by all the young girls in town. But Flo seemed happy, and her troubles with that girl Doreen seemed far behind her.

As for me, despite the strife between Sun and me, I believed we would marry. Everyone in Clark's Town expected it; it was only a matter of time. Maybe Sun was saving for a wedding, so I stayed patient. I had worked hard and given him all I could—dressed him in fine clothes, made sure he looked respectable. But when weeks passed with no word from him, I began to worry. I went to the house he rented to check on him.

The place was empty.

Everything was gone—the furniture, the clothes, the shoes I had given him. Not a trace of Sun remained in the room where we'd shared so many passionate nights. He had walked out of my life without a word.

I learned, several weeks later, that Sun had married another woman—a girl from Kinloss. The entire town was stunned. Everyone had expected him to marry me, perhaps even more than I had. I wept. I hated him. And I hated myself for being such a fool. I had loved a man who had never loved me.

The last night I saw him, he slept at my house. The very next morning, he married someone else.

Sun Brown Virgo had been much younger than I was. I had supported him, given him money so he wouldn't have to work. And in the end, like the others before him, he took what I gave and left. I came to accept that I would always be Vera Wallace. I was a beautiful woman, confident enough to know I could have had any man I wanted —but not one of them wanted me enough to stay.

17

KIDNAPPED

VERA

Life as a grandmother brought such joy, for I was a young granny. By the time little Bill was two years old, I was just forty-two, and since his father hardly visited, I looked forward to every moment I could spend with the boy. Flo's new man seemed loyal, but I remained skeptical of the man everyone called Keith Longmore, though his real name was McEwan. Keith was pleasant enough —always smiling—but I could never fully trust that sincere grin of his. Flo's man provided for her, but some of his closest friends were women, and while my daughter had no issue with this, I did.

Bill's father knew about Flo's relationship with Keith, and for that reason alone, I was glad this man had come into my child's life, despite my doubts about his smile. But I'd seen it in Johnson's eyes—the way he looked at my daughter. There was jealousy there. Mischief, even. Even Ma Jane had sensed it. It was Keith who advised Flo against sending the boy to spend time with his father, and when Flo came to me asking what she should do, I became so angry. How dare this man, who had only just entered her life, advise her not to send the child to stay with his father? I went to Keith and told him off. In his defence, Flo's man explained that he found it strange—after not visiting much —that the father suddenly wanted to take the boy for two weeks.

"Im nah guh bring im back!" Keith said.

But I allowed my distrust of Keith to cloud my judgment, and I told Flo there was nothing wrong with letting the boy spend some time with his father. I later realized Keith had been right, and I had been wrong...

Bill must have been two, maybe almost three, when Johnson took him. Flo was pregnant with her second child by then. The policeman had said he wanted to take the boy for two weeks, but he never brought him back. After weeks of hearing nothing from him, we went to the police station. Those devils gave us nothing—they said Goskel Johnson was no longer with the department. I wept for days. But what I felt could never compare to what my daughter had to endure, for she had lost her child to a vengeful, vindictive man.

Johnson must have known the pain he caused—not just to Flo, but to the entire family. We were all sad and worried. Lela and my other sisters came when they heard the news, and as weeks turned into months, we wondered if we'd ever see little Bill again...

Flora

THE LOSS OF MY ONLY CHILD WAS UNBEARABLE, FOR HE WAS ALIVE— stolen by the man who was supposed to love him. It felt as though my insides were ripped away, leaving me incomplete. I was no longer a whole woman, for a part of me was gone. I never heard from Goskel again. After months of waiting and searching for my son, I felt it was impossible to find him, for the police protected their own. Mama and I went to the station, spoke with the officer in charge, but he sat behind his desk staring at us as though it were a crime to seek the man who had stolen my child. I saw no compassion in his eyes when he told us that he had no idea where Goskel had taken my son. I couldn't sleep at night. Though Keith was supportive, concerned, and did all he could to help find my son, I went to bed weeping, wondering if Bill was alright —if he had been fed, if he was warm. Goskel had known nothing of his habits—that he liked to fall asleep with his bottle in his hand, though it was always empty. He never knew the songs that soothed him or how to rock him to sleep. Bill needed his mother. He needed me.

Goskel had come from the Parish of St. Thomas. At first, Mama and I traveled to Kingston, hoping to find him at the local police station, but he couldn't be found. It seemed he had indeed resigned from the police force. As we made our way back to Clark's Town on the crowded bus, winding along treacherous roads, I sat next to Mama—she had the window, as she always suffered from claustrophobia. I was silent, barely able to speak. My mind was consumed with questions, wondering why Goskel had done this, trying to comprehend why a father would take his child away from his mother. The bus seemed to creak and groan as it climbed higher, the view below a dangerous precipice—rocky, bushy, deadly. Each time I glanced over the edge, a cold fear gripped me. Even Mama cried out, "Lawd Jesus!" as we passed a particularly steep drop. She mopped sweat from her brow with her handkerchief. But still, my thoughts were fixed on Goskel. Why had he taken Bill away? Then, as if a fog lifted, I realized the truth—it wasn't that he loved the child so much. Goskel had taken Bill to punish me. That's when it all made sense. He had other children, surely, but it wasn't them he wanted. It was me. He had taken my son to hurt me, to take away what I loved most because I had found Keith.

I mentioned this to Mama, but she said nothing, her chin lifting slightly in quiet defiance. She hadn't approved of my relationship with Keith, and I knew it.

Four months passed after Bill was taken, and still no word from Goskel. But then, Herman, Keith's younger brother, found my son. I'm not sure how Herman and his friend discovered where Goskel was staying, but they brought me to Kingston. My heart raced as I stood by the gate, calling out for Goskel Johnson. Herman had gone over the plan repeatedly on the way. "Flo, mek sure yuh tek di child, then tell im from di road seh yuh deh guh home wid im. Dat way im cyan seh yuh kidnap im." My thoughts swirled. I was afraid.

Suddenly, I saw him—my son—walking out of the front door and coming towards me. I rushed to him, scooped him up, and held him tight, my tears soaking his little face. And then I heard Herman, his voice urgent from the road, "Flo, bring im outa di yard... cum!"

I still stood there, cradling Bill, weeping. Then, like a shadow, Goskel appeared, looming over us beneath the hot sun. He stared at me, his eyes cold. "Go back in di house, Bill," he commanded. And just like that, my baby turned and walked away, leaving me standing there, heartbroken once again.

I left Kingston that day in tears, feeling worse than I had when I arrived. I had seen my son, held him, kissed his face—and then he was gone again. What pained me most was the memory of his eyes, those soft brown eyes, staring up at me as his father led him back inside. The sound of his cries as the door closed behind him haunts me still.

The months that followed were painful. Though I had settled down with Keith, the emptiness of losing Bill never left me. I gave birth to my second son, Keith's first child, Wayne, in June of 1964. The labor was quick, but I'll never forget the look on Keith's face when I presented him with his son. It hurt more than I could ever put into words. Keith saw the pain in me, or maybe he felt it too. I couldn't help but feel robbed—cheated. Bill had turned three the month before, and I had no idea how he had spent his day. Did his father even remember it was his birthday?

I gave Keith his second son, Courtney, in April of 1966, just a month before Bill's fifth birthday. Rumours started to spread in Clark's Town that I might lose my job at the post office, being an unmarried woman with children. I knew Keith loved me, and I loved him. Even though there were whispers that he would leave me once I had his children, I continued to love him. I didn't ask him to marry me—I never would.

Keith, too, was in a difficult position. His friends advised him to marry me, and though he had considered it, he wasn't ready. He needed to be sure. Keith had come from a broken home—his mother had left, and he'd ended up homeless before being fostered by Jacob Longmore. I understood his past, and I never pressured him.

Courtney was born at Falmouth Hospital. Afterward, Keith made arrangements for us to move to Bottom Town with his foster parents, Mr. and Mrs. Longmore.

Keith and I were married on December 17, 1967—just four months after I gave birth to our fourth son, Garth. Mr. and Mrs. Longmore moved to Hyde soon after, and Keith came to me one day and simply asked, "Yuh waan married?" I said yes. It was that simple. He sent me to Miss Nennen, the dressmaker, and to Miss Eva Anderson's store for the other items I needed. We were a happy family of five, but the grief of losing my first child still tore at me, deep inside.

18

MA JANE
VERA

I had met a new man, one named Morris Belford. At the time, I was living at Aunt Emma's. We weren't really family, but everyone called her that. She had a son named Coolie Davis and a daughter named Alice. I was renting a room from Aunt Emma; she had two rooms, so she lived in one, and I lived in the other.

That old woman always woke early to sweep her yard. I often found myself grumbling under my breath that Aunt Emma was up long before the roosters crowed, the first sound I'd hear each morning, pulling me from my sleep, was the scrape of her broom against the dirt.

Aunt Emma lived in Top Town, not far from the main road. It was a quiet place, but back then, when I met Morris, I knew he wasn't mine to have, for he was with another woman. This was long before Flo gave birth to her second son, Wayne. I had first met Morris the year before. From the moment we crossed paths, I could tell he had eyes for me, and I knew I wanted him too.

Vera

I KNEW MORRIS WAS MINE THE MOMENT OUR EYES MET. I SAW THE SAME fire in him that I felt burning within me. I was modest, he was shy, but I flirted with him, knowing I could have him. Morris Belford was the man I wanted, and it never mattered to me that he was living with another woman, that he was father to two young children. In fact, his son, Junior, and my grandson, Wayne, were born in the same year. I'd seen the other woman—she hardly seemed deserving of him.

I was forty-seven, and Morris was ten years younger. His body was lean, muscular, and his waistline so small it made me want to starve myself—though I wasn't fat. Morris had the thinnest of moustaches above full lips, and his complexion was a light brown, almost like a white man, though not as pale. His smile was pleasant, and in it, I saw desire. I knew right away that he wanted me.

I first met him while he was working with the Chinaman, Oswald Chin, on a building project. At the same time, I was also working with Mr. Chin. One day, I passed by as Morris worked, hammering nails into the roof, and I heard him singing. Morris loved to sing. I loved to sing. His voice was almost a soprano—far from the typical baritone—and his passion for music only deepened my desire for him.

Morris was a carpenter by trade, and he owned a small plot of land where he grew his own food and sugar cane. There seemed to be nothing he couldn't do. He was building his own home in the district of Hyde, and he was a master at making furniture.

I'd seen his woman a few times before—nothing special in my eyes. But I wasn't deterred when I sensed that Morris wanted me as much as I wanted him.

I felt no remorse the day he accepted my invitation to dinner. I had cooked the best meal I could, but when he didn't eat a single bite, I was puzzled and sorely vexed. I had set the table, made drinks, and put all my effort into preparing the evening. But what I learned that night shocked me: Morris didn't trust most women, and he rarely ate food they prepared.

The man was superstitious, and my anger quickly melted when he shared the story of how another woman had once betrayed him.

"Mi come home early to raasclaat—"

"Morris, stop cussing!" I clapped my hands over my ears, refusing to believe he could be anything like the other men from my past.

"V, mi catch di dutty gyal wid har pum-pum over mi food to rockstone mi mouth."

I gasped. I had heard such terrible tales of what some women would do to keep a man. I turned away, disgusted. How could any woman do such a thing? Pulling down her drawers and stooping over a man's food?

I glanced back at the table where I had spent hours preparing the meal. The thought of eating now felt impossible. But then, Morris took my hand. His carpenter's hands weren't soft, but something about his touch made my body shiver. He must have seen the goosebumps rise on my arms.

He pulled the curtains for privacy, drawing me close to him. I could feel my breasts press against the firmness of his chest. Morris pressed his cheek to mine, and then he did the strangest thing. He began to sing one of my favourite songs. It took me back thirty years, to the dances I used to attend...

"*Everybody, everybody... there's a scandal in this town... with a gal named Stella Blossom and a fella by the name of Rufus Brown...*"

I leaned my face on his shoulder and laughed when he sang that same verse again, but this time, he sang '*Vera Wallace*' instead of '*Stella Blossom*', and '*Morris Belford*' instead of '*Rufus Brown*'. I couldn't help but join in, and as our voices blended together, I knew I had him.

"*Oh, my Morris, hold me tight... oh, squeeze me with all yuh might...*"

We crooned Lionel Belasco's Oh Rufus, Hold Me Tight, in our own way, dancing until the moment our lips met. There was no need for us to sing anymore.

The dinner had long gone cold after we made love. Morris ate it still. And in that moment, I knew: she'd lost him. The other woman was no longer a part of his life. I had found myself a new man.

But it took years before I was certain Morris would be all mine. Our relationship had ended several times. We left each other for long periods, and in those months, I became involved with others—if only to forget the man I loved so deeply. But it was impossible. No matter how hard I tried, I could never forget Morris Belford, the love of my life.

———————

———————

———————

Vera

ONE OF THE MOST DREADFUL DAYS OF MY LIFE BEGAN WITH HEAVY RAINS. It was the third week of September. Flo's new son, Wayne, was only three months old. My belly ached each time I saw the pain in Flo's eyes, for she hadn't been the same since Johnson ran off with Bill—my first grandson. Bill had just begun uttering his first words when that devil took him away. I couldn't help but ask myself—and God—why men carried such wickedness in their hearts.

I visited Ma Jane and Flo a week before that rainy day. That night, I sat with Ma Jane for a long while, for she was getting on in age. It felt strange somehow, seeing her so fragile. My granny had been strong most of her life, but at ninety-five, it was as if she'd grown old overnight. She had become calmer in her twilight years, though she still hadn't given up smoking her pipe—or eating the ashes. I never understood why my granny ate burnt tobacco ashes.

Flo still lived with Ma Jane, even though she was with her new man, Keith. She wouldn't move to Bottom Town with him until after

Courtney, their second child, was born. Flo and I had been raised by Ma Jane like sisters, but that evening, we sat with our granny as mother and daughter. So many memories flooded back as I sat at the edge of her bed. Her green eyes sparkled in the lamplight. She smiled at me, and I looked at her, heart aching at the sight of this once indomitable woman now so frail. But in her eyes, that fire still burned—relentless, full of will.

I took Ma Jane's hand and squeezed it. Again, she smiled.

"V," she said, "Ah deh feel it."

She took a deep breath, pressing her palm against her chest. She had long suffered from terrible chest pains.

"Nuh worry, Ma Jane," I said. "Yuh soon get betta…"

She smiled at me again.

After promising to visit again soon, I left Ma Jane, Flo, and the rest of the household behind.

The following Thursday, the rain came, and it seemed it would never cease. Later that day, a message came: Ma Jane had gotten worse. She had been asking for me. I dropped what I was doing at work and rushed over. I walked through the gate, soaked to the skin, and entered the house—only to be told that Ma Jane had just passed, only moments before I arrived.

I crumbled to the wooden floor and wept.

"Ma Jane," I cried. "Ma Jane! Yuh couldn't wait till mi cum, Ma Jane!"

Her body was still warm when I touched her.

Ma Jane was dead.

And I, the one everyone called her pearl, was too late.

Her body was kept on ice, upon her bed, as was the custom. The nights that followed were filled with singing, drinking, and games out in the yard, right up until the day she was laid to rest beside Tata Joe, beneath the breadfruit trees.

I sang at my granny's funeral. I had always loved to sing, and she had always loved to hear me. I stood among the many whose lives she'd touched. The entire yard was full. Some had been whipped by her at their parents' behest; others had been fed, healed, or taken in when they had no place else to go. Many came simply because they remembered the way her emerald eyes bulged when she disapproved of them. Others were brought into the world by her hands.

Mary Jane Hall was gone—but not forgotten.

Vera

THAT SAME YEAR, AFTER MA JANE'S DEATH, I RECEIVED TERRIBLE NEWS about Morris. We weren't yet living together, but I had committed myself to the man I loved—waiting patiently for him to leave the other woman.

I was at home when word came: Morris had been arrested. I rushed out immediately, heart pounding, for something awful had happened.

Morris had chopped a man with a machete.

Only God saved the man's life.

It had been the end of the week—pay day. Morris and another man had argued over money, right there on the job site. The quarrel escalated into a fight, and in the heat of it, Morris reached for his machete and struck the man.

I arrived just in time to see Morris being taken away, his face swollen, his body bruised and bloodied. But the man he'd injured was worse—his blood stained the ground where they had fought. The dirt was dark and wet with it.

Morris spent six months in prison for chopping that man, and I waited for him.

I did everything I could. I visited him. I supported him. I loved him still.

I can't say whether he was right in what he did. But I do believe that man should never have provoked Morris.

19

MORRIS BELFORD
VERA

My daughter's life flourished, and her womb was blessed—one child after another. Not only did my one child conceive with ease, but she carried each pregnancy to term without a single complication.

Keith was a lucky man.

Yet there were times I wondered if he even realized that my Flo was one of a kind—a good, loyal woman. I'd watch him and understand why so many women were drawn to him. He treated my daughter with the respect she deserved, and he was a good provider. Still, I remained cautious of this man with the most sincere of smiles.

Yes, he was pleasant. Yes, he was respectful.

But there was one woman—Sydney Brady, his best friend.

She and Keith had become... close. Too close. I hadn't always seen the failings in my own relationships—nor had I wanted to—but I was a mother, and I had no qualms voicing my disapproval when it came to the bond between my child's husband and another woman.

Flo was furious when word reached her that I'd been making remarks about her man.

"Mama," she said, "Wah mek yuh nuh stop from chat 'bout Keith an' Sydoney?"

She told me how much she trusted him. Said Keith would never keep another woman.

"Every man ah grindsman," I said.

Flo looked at me like I'd slapped her—shocked that I still doubted her husband. And Keith? well, he'd heard what I'd said too. I could always see it in his eyes—the quiet anger. But still, he remained respectful.

In January of 1969, Flo gave Keith his daughter, Erica.

———

———

———

Vera

BY THE TIME FLO'S ONLY DAUGHTER, ERICA—NICKNAMED SHAWN— turned one, Morris and his woman were no longer together. She had taken the two children back to south Trelawny, near Albert Town. And though it was clear Morris missed them dearly, especially his boy, Clement, I felt no pity for the woman.

I had won him.

His children were not mine to care for.

Of course, I could never admit this to Morris—for what he didn't know couldn't hurt him. It was Morris Belford I wanted, not another woman's baggage. Besides, I was already a granny. My one child was the mother of five.

But life has a way of humbling us when we're not fully sincere. Those two children eventually came to live with us permanently after I moved into Morris's house in Hyde.

And no matter how I tried, I could never accept them.

Peggy, the girl, was quiet and respectful enough—both children were, really. But I could hardly stand Morris's boy. He was mouthy, even as a child, always talking back. And it wasn't just his words—it was his eyes. In those eyes, I saw her. His mother. I saw her in his face, in his soul. And I couldn't bring myself to be the gentle stepmother Morris imagined me to be.

The boy knew I didn't like him. I saw it. Felt it.

Peggy was expected to stay by my side and learn all the things a girl needed to become a woman. Neither of us relished the idea. She clearly cared little for the woman who had replaced her mother and shattered her happy home.

And each time I caught that sidelong glance from her—she wasn't even ten yet—I wanted to tell her the truth: her parents were never meant to last. If it hadn't been me, it would've been some other woman.

So, while Morris's daughter tolerated my teachings and likely wished me dead (for I could feel those darting eyes in my back), I watched Morris pour himself into his son.

He taught the boy to count, to do his sums long before school ever started. He also showed him the craft of carpentry. And the boy learned fast.

They never called me "Mother." They called me Miss Vera. And that was enough. I was nearly fifty and had already raised my one child —who, by the way, was enjoying motherhood more with each passing year.

By December 1970, Flo was pregnant again.

She gave birth to Ricardo—Ricky—in August of 1971. He was only three months old, still at her breast, when she conceived again. In September 1972, she had her seventh and last child: Gregory.

She would've had eight altogether, for Garth had been a twin.

Still, even after all her blessings, my daughter remained incomplete. Because by the time little Greg—her wash belly—came into the world, it had been nine long, painful years since that man took Bill away.

We'd never heard from the policeman again.

And though Flo bore six more children after her first was stolen, she was never the same.

20

THE VOICE THAT CALLS ME HOME
VERA

Long before Ma Jane died—back when the Yahweh church was built on our land at Top Town—I'd always felt close to God.

There were times in my life when everything went wrong. Still, even then, I felt something—like a fire shut up in my bones.

Ma Jane and I often visited Bredda Nattie's revival church down in Bottom Town, but even before that, as a girl, my sisters and I had attended Saint Michael's Anglican Church. Those days were painful for me, mostly because of old Krueger Milliner and his long white beard.

But God always has a plan for us, even when we don't have time to think of Him.

It was a hot Sunday when I found God. But really, it was He who found me.

He had always known me.

That day, Flo was home. It was before Bill was born. I've always loved music—loved the swell of a hymn, the rise and fall of voices, the thrill of drums and tambourines. The Yahweh church was in full session, and the hymn they sang that afternoon gave me chills.

I left what I was doing and walked to the window. I stood outside, just watching. But then the world around me vanished. It was as if I lost all control of my body. I was drawn into the church—not by my own will, but by God's. By Yahweh's will.

That afternoon I spoke in tongues, lifting my hands to the heavens. I praised the Creator for blessings I hadn't even asked for. I wept. I sang. I thanked Him in a language only He could understand.

I didn't fully acknowledge it then, but I knew He had changed me.

Still—I was far from perfect. I was only human.

Ma Jane and I kept attending Bredda Nattie's church. Revival wasn't like the Yahweh church, or the Baptist, or even the Anglican. People say revival was born in Africa—a revival from dead works unto righteousness.

The revival people wore turbans—every colour under the sun. They beat old drums made of stretched goat skin, rocked their bodies and chanted, and sang hymns that reached down into the bones.

Whenever I visited Leader Allen's church, I felt like running. The Holy Ghost would grip me.

"God a-go bruk yuh foot dem," old Ma Betsie used to warn. "Yuh cyan run from Holy Ghost! Yuh cyan run too far."

I never paid her much mind. Her granddaughter, Estlyn Kelly—Miss We-we—we worked together at Miss Chin's and Oswald Chin's shop. She was always nearby to hear her granny tell lecture me about my salvation.

I always felt revival was my true calling, but I was disobedient. I liked my life. I feared change.

But one Sunday, while visiting Leader Nathaniel Allen again, a young preacher came to the pulpit—a tall, slim man named Eric Guthrie. His church was in Hyde, not far from where Morris and I lived.

That day, the church was full—even Flo was there. She'd since been baptized and was now the church secretary.

The moment Leader Guthrie started singing of Zion, I felt those chills again.

The elders sang ancient hymns and the congregation moved as one. I watched sinners thrash on the ground. Feet stomped against the floor like the sound of an army marching.

The floor had been polished red.

At the centre of the church was a table with flowers, water, and candles. On the red floor surrounding it were symbols—words in Hebrew I couldn't read, stars and letters drawn in white. They called that area the seal. And it had been written up by one Brother Saunders.

Leader Guthrie and Leader Allen walked upon it, stomping their feet—one man tall, the other short. Leader Guthrie held a ruler, Leader Allen his staff. They spoke in tongues and dialects I had never heard in my life.

Something overtook me.

I turned to flee, but my knees buckled. I lifted my hands and cried out. My mouth filled with words I didn't recognize. My own voice echoed in my head.

I moved toward the seal, drawn again—not by my will.

No one touched me. I stood before the leaders, arms raised, and spoke to heaven with authority I never knew I had.

Later in the service, the church lifted a chorus, and that song became one of my lifelong favourites.

All voices blended together—the saved, the sinners, drunkards and thieves, people from every walk of life. The churchyard had overflowed with them.

Drums rattled, tambourines jingled, hands clapped and feet stomped in rhythm.

And we sang:

It is the voice that calls me home,
Up from the hills,
The rising sun,
I hear it say...come onto me,
It is that voice that calls me home...

THE RHYTHM OVERTOOK MY FEET. I RAN AROUND THE SEAL—NOT TO escape, but to rejoice.

That day, I got saved.

And on a Sunday in 1974, I was baptized and became a member of The New Testament Church of Christ the Redeemer under Leader Eric Guthrie.

I was one of many candidates that morning. We were taken to the river. I wore white. My head was wrapped in a white turban.

Pastor Guthrie took my hands, clasped them before my chest, and I closed my eyes. I heard the voices of the brethren singing by the riverside. He lowered me into the water—buried the old Vera Wallace—and raised me again, changed.

There was a young man who was baptized with me that day. His name was Stanley Benbow. He couldn't have been more than thirteen, but in his eyes I saw conviction.

That day, I became Sister Wallace.

I was fifty-one years old.

And I had no idea that most of the trials in my life had only just begun.

21

CANADA
VERA

As I had cared for and raised nearly all the Chinese children in Clark's Town, nursing my grandchildren came easy, for it had been I who looked after Flo's children when the time came for her to give birth. Six children were more than a handful for Flo, with Keith in Canada on a work visa. He had left when Flo was with child and returned in time for Ricky's birth in 1971.

When the wash belly, Greg, was born the following year, however, Keith had been away again. So father and youngest son met at the airport upon his return, when the babe was just a few months old.

I'd had my reservations about the man—my son-in-law—but he was a good father. A good husband. And I admit now, in my old age, that Keith had been good to his family and to me, for he treated me as though I were his own mother. He adored my child.

What else could a mother ask for than a good man for her daughter? But I'd always said to Flo that I feared God no longer made men like her Keith... or Daddy, as I'd ended up calling him.

I was at home one day in 1974, washing Morris's clothes, when Flo and the children paid a visit. Wayne had been ten years old, and Courtney eight. Garth was seven, Shawn—the only girl—was five,

Ricky, or Baboo, as Mr. Longmore had nicknamed him, was just three. Greg, the wash belly, was two years old.

The older children bellowed my name in unison. "Granny! Wy-wa!"

Wy-wa was my other name for granny.

They came running toward me and fell upon the washed clothes, splashing soapsuds everywhere.

"Courtney!"

Flo had Greg in her arms, those huge eyes scrutinizing the world around him with serious suspicion, for he seldom smiled and had been nicknamed the judge by some fool who must have had little to do with his time.

Flo's third child, Courtney, was full of energy—a strong-willed, handsome boy who hardly listened to his mother. But Courtney had been Jacob Longmore's pet, just as I'd been Ma Jane's pearl. The boy could do no wrong in his adopted grandfather's eyes.

The children, and everyone else, had grown to know Mr. Longmore as Banka; his wife, Deleta Longmore, was Miss Del. Wayne had been Miss Del's favourite, for he was Keith's firstborn.

Little Ricky clung to Flo's side, nearly in tears, for he so loved to weep. And Shawn, the only girl child, had always been one of many moods. She stood close to her mother, observing me as if to challenge me to a stare-down, hardly willing to share the attention of her protectors—her brothers.

The three older boys showered my face with kisses, and I playfully splashed their faces with soapy water, which brought loud giggles. I will admit that I detested spanking children, for I had always been a playful woman.

After Flo managed to get the children to go off playing with Morris's two, she sat next to me with the bulb-eyed wash belly on her lap.

"Mama," Flo said. She was apprehensive, choosing her words carefully.

"Mama... mi deh guh a Canada."

I immediately stopped my washing. I felt I knew what words would come next. But I was shocked and hurt when Flo told me the children would be left in Miss Del's care. I as their granny.

I was the one who made them laugh.

I was the one they called Wy-wa. But Flo decided to leave them with Keith's adopted parents.

Several weeks later, I went with the children to the airport to bid my only child goodbye. I wept, for though I had never set foot on an aircraft, I feared the worst. The airplane taxied away, preparing to take Flo far across the waters to another land, and around me, as I dabbed my tears with a white hanky, her children waved without much understanding.

They hardly had a clue that it could be years before they saw their mother again. But I knew.

I saw the tiny image of Flo waving her white handkerchief, her face framed by a square pane of glass. And then she was gone.

But my house was no longer a haven. And soon the warmth of family gave way to a storm I partly stirred myself.

Over the next several months, things between Morris and me changed. We were always in conflict. One of the major issues was his son, Clement—or Junior, as he was called.

The boy and I could never get along, for he had never made the effort to accept me. And I will admit—he was the only child I ever enjoyed spanking.

There were times when I did so for no reason at all, simply because he was there in my presence and I could hardly tolerate looking at him, seeing his mother in his eyes.

The boy was mouthy, so I would break a switch from the hibiscus hedge, strip off the leaves, and whip him good. And even as he wept there, seated on the ground in the kitchen, he still talked back—threatening to tell his father I had hit him without cause.

But when Morris came home, I made certain I reached him first.

I wept. I told him how much I loved him. I warned him that I didn't know how much more of the boy's insolence I could endure.

I even made up stories—lies. Told Morris things the boy had never done or said, and watched him get another whipping for it.

And for what I'd done, for all the damage I had caused, I saw in Junior's eyes that he hated me for it.

But I had to teach him a good lesson. Show him who held the power. I told Morris those lies right there before the boy, just so he could see it was I his father believed—and not him.

And the way he looked at me that day—like he'd never forget—I see it still.

———————

———————

———————

Flora

I WAS HAPPY TO BE WITH MY HUSBAND IN TORONTO, BUT I WAS HOMESICK and couldn't endure being away from my children. My youngest was just two years old, while my oldest, Bill—who had been thirteen, well on his way to becoming a man—was still hidden from me. I wept at night, even as I worked caring for the children of others in a land so far from the world I'd known all my life.

I had told Keith many times that I wanted to return home. I didn't know whether Bill was dead or alive. I worried that he had forgotten me after all these years, for he had not yet turned three when his father took him away.

As the months dragged on and summer days drifted by, news began to trickle in from Jamaica of a conflict brewing between Mama and Miss Del. Mama wrote me her version of events, claiming the children hated staying with Miss Del, complaining daily that she mistreated them.

Miss Del wrote letters too. Sometimes she even called, voicing her own grievances—that Mama constantly undermined her authority, always reminding everyone she was their grandmother.

I couldn't take the complaints any longer. By December of the same year I arrived in Canada, I returned home to Jamaica to resolve the matter.

Flights had been cheap, and I went against Keith's advice, staying in Jamaica for just one week. I hadn't told Mama or Miss Del I was coming.

The night I arrived, I approached the gate of the Longmore residence under a dark sky speckled with millions of stars. I heard how Banka spoke to my children, and it made me angry.

Miss Del, her brother Mass Harry, and Banka were seated on the veranda. They must have seen the way I marched in—must have known I'd overheard them shouting at my children and witnessed my anger.

But I was quickly calmed at the sight of my babies. I drew them all close to me and wept.

After speaking with the older children and with Mama, I decided it was best to meet with the parties involved. Mama accused Miss Del of keeping her grandchildren from her, saying Miss Del would get angry and forbid them to visit, even though they lived so close.

I confronted Miss Del with Mama present. She refused to address the matter. Keith's adopted mother—a well-educated woman and principal at Hyde's Basic School—simply looked away into the distance. Her large, bulb-like eyes avoided my gaze.

"Duh what yuh want to duh, Flo," she said.

That was all.

I made arrangements to rent a home not far from where Mama and Mass Morris lived. Mama would take care of the children.

Miss Del was not pleased that I moved them from her house. And instead of resolving the conflict, I feared my visit only worsened the already fragile relationship between the two women. It was evident there had always been jealousy and animosity between them.

But I did what I felt was best for my children.

I left for Canada feeling somewhat relieved. Still, my week in

Jamaica had been painful. I couldn't set foot on that island without wondering what had become of my first child.

I did the only thing I could.

I had known Goskel's mother, Miss Adrienne, and every year I sent her Christmas cards and birthday cards for Bill. I had no idea if he ever saw them. I sent them to his granny, the only address I knew.

But whether she passed the letters to Bill—or to his father—I couldn't say.

I remembered Miss Adrienne well. She had been terrified of her own son.

Keith and I had visited her months after Bill had been taken. We went during a time when we knew Goskel Johnson was in America. That day, Miss Adrienne wept. She said she wanted to help us, but couldn't say where Bill was staying.

She feared her son would never forgive her—that he would cut off the financial support he provided.

But Goskel's sister had also been there that day. She promised Keith she would keep in touch, even after we moved to Canada.

And it was Bill's aunt who eventually helped reunite me with my long-lost child.

Vera

CARING FOR MY GRANDCHILDREN HAD BEEN A TASK ALL ITS OWN. AT first, the children stayed in the middle room at Morris's house, but Flo insisted a separate house be rented for them. That left me—a working woman of over fifty—managing two households. It was difficult to leave six children alone in one house at night, but Morris needed me at the other.

Morris never said it outright, but I never felt he liked that I was suddenly caring for six grandchildren along with his two. Still, he had been good with the children. He was a man with a hilarious sense of humour, always laughing and saying the silliest things. Many times, I had to slap his shoulder and say, "Morris!" because he'd say things not fit for young ears.

But Morris never cursed in front of the children. He just said things they couldn't have understood. He was a clever man, always eager to share what he knew.

His boy, Junior, continued to be a thorn in my side—and I made sure I was one in his. At nearly twelve, he had become more insolent. I made sure Morris trusted my word over his, because I saw how much he adored that boy. I whipped him during the day while his father was out and made sure he got it again when Morris came home. Junior feared his father.

The girl, on the other hand, knew her place. But I was no fool—I knew she despised me. She was a girl, soon to be a woman, and I saw the hate in her eyes. Her mother had never liked me, and I hated the woman so deeply that I could barely stand being near her children. God alone knew why Morris insisted they live with us.

Still, I welcomed the quiet when they were gone. During school breaks, Peggy and Junior usually stayed with their mother. I enjoyed those few weeks of peace, and so did Morris.

As soon as he came home, and after I had fed him, he would shut the curtains and the door and pull me close. My man would play all his favourite 8-track tapes and vinyl records, because Morris loved to dance.

He had always been a jealous man—especially of my long-time friend, Larry Brown.

Larry and I had grown up together. Long before I had Flo, we sang and danced on stage during the war years. Larry and I were never lovers, though he was a handsome man. He never once put question to me. We danced close, sang even closer, and while there were always rumours about Larry—whispers about his lack of interest in women—none of it mattered to me.

But Morris could never get past it. My friendship with Larry stayed in his mind.

So at home, Morris danced with me until our feet were sore, and he sang until his voice failed him—all because of Larry Brown.

Morris Belford believed he was the best singer in the whole world, but he was not as good as I.

At night, after my six grandchildren were asleep, I'd lock up the house and go home to Morris. We'd sit together under the stars and sing—just the two of us beneath the sky.

22

THE LOST LAMB
VERA

During my younger years, I learned early not to care what others thought of me. So from the days when I used to go to dances and sing on stage, I held my head high. Back then, many of my rivals—the women—feared I would snatch their men away.

There's no doubt I loved the parties and the dances. I'll admit, I wasted many years living that life. Looking back now, I know I shouldn't have. But I found God in time, and He changed my life.

The women I once danced beside hadn't changed, though—they, too, called themselves children of God.

After I got saved and baptized, there were still years of song and dance trapped inside me. So when I went to church and the Spirit of the Lord fell upon me, those same women would laugh. I was new to this life with God, and my party days were long behind me. But music was music. The rattle of the drums and the blend of voices made me rejoice. That music moved me the same way the party music once did.

I didn't understand it all back then. But whenever I danced in the Spirit, it felt no different from the days when I swayed on stage in the arms of a handsome man. I spoke in tongues and rejoiced Sunday after

Sunday, but I still moved the old way—like the party girl I used to, hips swaying to Lionel Belasco's *Oh Rufus Hold Me Tight*.

They laughed. The church sisters giggled and whispered in the pews while I danced to the drums and raised my arms to heaven. Even my leader laughed.

But with all the talk, all the stares, I still walked into that little church every Sunday with my head held high. Because I was a lady.

They said I was too proud.

But Vera Wallace didn't care one bit.

———

———

———

Vera

AS I GREW SPIRITUALLY AND LEARNED THE WAYS OF THE CHURCH, THE gossip about me continued. Though the way I moved to the music had changed, the church members still found something to whisper about —huddled in little clusters like a flock of blackbirds.

It was around that time I learned of Morris's indiscretions. After he began having an affair with the sister of a woman named Bunny, the entire district of Hyde knew what was happening in our home. Morris was a quiet man. He had never raised his hand to me. But he loved girls. And his unfaithfulness only grew worse—so bad I could no longer endure it.

He promised he'd never leave me, yet never once admitted to the things he did behind my back with those women. We argued often. I needed him to confess what I already knew—that he was a cheat. But Morris never did.

I would walk into church and hear the whispers—utterances of that woman's name. There were comments too. That I, a child of God, was living in sin with a man who wouldn't marry me. That I was only reaping what I'd sown, since I had taken Morris from another woman.

Still, I held my head high. But deep inside, it pained me. I feared that after giving Morris my all—after caring for him, loving him—he would go against his promise and leave.

The comments kept coming:

"Miss Vera inna church an' she nuh married."

"Mass Morris nah married har."

All this, I endured. But it was the fear of losing Morris I couldn't bear. There were times I believed the end had come.

I left Morris several times over a few months. I had another place where I stayed with my grandchildren. When Flo found out about the back and forth between Morris and me, she decided she didn't want her children living in that kind of instability. My daughter wrote and told me the children should go back to live with the Longmores.

I can't say I was pleased. But the arrangement gave me space to try and salvage my relationship with Morris.

The day I brought the six children to Miss Del's house, I saw satisfaction in her eyes. A slight smile at the corner of her mouth. She sat there on the veranda and said nothing. Only Banka seemed pleased to see the children again.

Miss Del didn't show joy for having the children—not the kind a grandmother might show. Her joy was for the victory. My loss.

She'd always taken in children without homes, and made a point of it. But her love of money was no secret—at least not to me. I knew that her reason for wanting the children had little to do with love, and everything to do with the financial support Flo and Keith would provide.

Vera

THE NEWS CAME ON A WEDNESDAY EVENING WHILE I WAS BUSY MAKING supper for Morris. It was Pauline—Lela's daughter, the one we all call Hope—who brought word that Bill was coming home.

Somehow, Johnson's sister had managed to reach out to Keith and Flo in Canada, and just like that, the arrangements were made. My lost grandson was returning.

I dropped everything. The pot still simmering on the stove, I headed straight for Miss Del's. As I walked up the lane toward the main Hyde road, my stomach weakened, and my vision blurred with tears. I hadn't seen Bill since he was just a toddler. And now, in the summer of 1976, the little boy taken from us by his father would be returning—not as a child, but as a young man.

In just a matter of days, I would be meeting my grandchild again— a teenager of fifteen. And it pained me to think... he might not remember his granny.

That evening, Miss Del, Banka, and I sat on the veranda and talked. I told them what I'd heard, explaining that since Bill's siblings were already living there, space would need to be made. Flo wanted all her children together again.

As I spoke, I noticed the greedy glint rise in Miss Del's large eyes.

Bill

I LEFT ST. THOMAS VERY EARLY THAT MORNING. IT WAS THE SUMMER OF 1976, and I knew the bus ride to Clark's Town would take several hours. The dew still clung to the grass and plants in my uncle's garden as I slipped out into the dawn. The sky was dark, and dogs barked somewhere in the distance—faint echoes of a town waking up to another hot, hectic day.

It was my uncle, Egbert—my father's brother—who dropped me off to catch the bus. I had stayed with his family for just over a year, until his wife, Aunt Ruby, decided it was time I left.

My father was Goskel Johnson, but no one ever used that name. To everyone, he was Johnny. I ran away from Johnny's house when I was thirteen and never looked back. The years before that were filled with beatings and coldness from a rotating door of stepmothers. Life got even harder after I ran, until I eventually found refuge with a group of Rastafarians. On the compound, I quickly took to their ways—refusing to cut my hair, eat pork, or even use salt in my food.

When Uncle Egbert found me on the streets, he took me in. Aunt Ruby, kind at first, grew tired. With six children of her own, I was just another mouth to feed. Johnny never sent support, even though he knew I was with his brother. Why would he? I'd disobeyed him by running away. I knew he'd never give a cent. Uncle Egbert knew it too.

But Aunt Ruby had her own ideas. She'd once lived in Clark's Town, and somehow she made arrangements to return me to my family. She wanted her household back the way it was before I arrived.

A few weeks before I left, I'd begun writing to my cousin Hope—Pauline. We hadn't met, or if we had when I was small, I didn't remember her. Still, we exchanged letters. And on the morning I left, as I boarded the bus and said goodbye to Uncle Egbert, a strange mix of apprehension and excitement filled me. By day's end, I would be back in Clark's Town—the place I had lived before Johnny took me. This time, I would live in the district of Hyde, with Mr. and Mrs. Longmore.

I sat alone on the bus, nervous and exhausted, with no idea what lay ahead. Everything I owned fit into one duffle bag. I'd even brought my makeshift aquarium—a jar of fish I refused to leave behind. I clutched it on my lap the entire trip. My appetite was gone. With every bus change, I drew closer to something I couldn't yet name—a new life, maybe even a home.

I found it strange that these strangers I was going to meet were my blood. My father had always said my mother was dead. He said it often enough that I eventually believed him. But I remembered Mommy. I was almost three when Johnny took me, and I had memories of the man called Keith, too—he'd taken care of us. Those memories stayed with me, the only ones I was allowed to keep. Johnny never spoke of Mommy unless to remind me she was gone.

But she wasn't gone. She was in Canada. Johnny had lied.

The thought of meeting six siblings I had never known tormented me. I was the eldest—at least, I was supposed to be. Hope had written their names to me, and I whispered them to myself as the bus rolled along: Wayne, Courtney, Garth, Erica, Ricky, and Greg. My five brothers and one sister—all from the same mother. My mother.

———

———

———

Vera

———

I SAT ON MISS DEL'S VERANDA FOR HOURS, AND IT SEEMED THE MORE I gazed up the road for my grandson, the longer it took for him to arrive. Miss Del and Banka were also seated outside, along with Miss Del's brother, Mass Harry. The children were there too—some on the veranda, others playing in the front yard behind the iron gate and the tall hibiscus hedge.

When I finally saw a figure appear at the top of the hill, just after the area where Grace Street crossed with Hyde Road, I was filled with joy. I had explained to the other children that their brother was coming home, though it seemed only the older ones understood. The gate creaked as Bill passed through and walked toward us. I couldn't help weeping as I slowly rose from the bench and stepped down to meet Flo's first child.

Miss Del and Banka remained seated, watching in silence, without emotion.

Bill was no longer the little boy I remembered playing at my feet some eleven or twelve years earlier—he was a man now, a stranger to me, yet still my daughter's child. I saw in his dark pupils that he had little memory of me, and as I embraced him, I wept. The love I carried for Flo's little boy had endured all those years, and in that moment, it felt as if he had never left.

"Bill," I said. "Is Granny...Granny Vera..."

He held back his tears, kept his emotions caged—he was a man now. It took some time to let him go. As I stepped back and looked at Flo's eldest son, I was struck: he had his father's face, but Flo's eyes. Even his smile bore Mr. Johnson's own white teeth, and it pained me to remember the hell that man had put us through. Bill's dark complexion was his father's, and he wore his black hair like a great plume atop his head. He was tall, slim, dressed in a brightly coloured shirt—almost psychedelic, like the coat of many colours Joseph had worn. His pants were faded, and the small duffel he carried bore the Adidas logo.

Bill looked at his six siblings in awe. Little Greg, the youngest, was just four. Wayne, the second eldest, was already twelve.

As we talked, I felt a slow-burning rage. That wicked man had told his own son that my only child—his mother—was dead. And through it all, the only thing Miss Del could comment on was the fact that my grandchild was a rasta. Her eyes never left his uncut hair.

Bill took long, lingering glances at his siblings, still stunned, for he'd never known they existed.

I stayed there for hours, temporarily forgetting Morris's home and the duties that waited there. Flo's lost lamb had returned.

Over the next several days, as my grandson and I spoke, I learned the truth—he had never received the letters or cards Flo had sent over the years. That wicked man had stolen them from him. Either he destroyed them, or Bill's other granny had never told him they came. But why would a father who'd stolen a child ever let him see letters from a mother he claimed was dead? In my gut, I knew it: Johnson and his mother destroyed those letters. They had stolen years we could never get back.

23

A FATHER'S CLAIM

Jacob Longmore (Banka)

Jacob Longmore sat in his favourite chair on the veranda, his machete laid across his lap. He'd already told the children to go inside and stay there. Someone was coming.

He positioned himself in a way that made it clear who was master of the house. Reaching for the file beside him, he tilted the already sharp blade and resumed the slow, deliberate motion of dragging the file along the edge—sharpening it further. The blade glistened in the sunlight.

Jacob glanced over at his wife, the woman he'd lived with for many years and simply called D.

Deleta—or Miss Del, as most others knew her—sat beside him, her eyes fixed on the distant road.

"Im deh cum, Jakey," she said.

Jacob looked up the road and saw the vehicle approaching the gate. It had to be Bill's father. He'd been warned the man was coming to take back his son—or at least, try to.

As the dark man pushed the gate open and the dog rose from the steps, barking, Jacob called softly to the animal. "Nib."

The dog stopped, but remained alert, eyes locked on the stranger as he made his way toward the veranda.

Jacob said nothing as the man stood there, legs apart, hands on his hips, staring at him and Miss Del. He didn't know the man personally, but he knew enough—he knew what the man had done to his adopted son's wife thirteen years earlier.

Jacob stayed silent. This was Johnson's moment to explain himself.

The man had come all the way from St. Thomas to claim his son— the same boy he'd taken from his mother at a tender age. But Bill was no longer a boy. He was fifteen now, and his mother had written Jacob and his wife, asking them to keep her son until she could come for him herself.

At last, Johnson spoke the words Jacob had been expecting.

"Mr. Longmore, mi come fi mi son, Bill."

Jacob didn't respond. He simply dragged the file slowly across the blade again, eyes never leaving the man.

He saw no fear in Johnson—this was a former police officer, after all.

Johnson explained that his son had run away from St. Thomas, and he'd come to take him back. Jacob calmly replied that the boy was in his care by his mother's written instruction, and that Bill would remain with them until she said otherwise.

Johnson left the yard, but Jacob turned to Miss Del and stated one fact: they had not seen the last of Goskel Johnson.

He was right.

Several hours later, Johnson returned with two police officers. He announced again that he had come to claim his son.

Jacob nodded to Miss Del. She went into the house and returned— not with Bill, but with a letter from Canada.

It was from Flo.

She had written to say that her son was to remain with Jacob and Deleta until she came to collect him herself. Calmly, Jacob told the officers the boy was well cared for, living happily with his six siblings.

After reading the letter and hearing the truth, the officers told Johnson there was nothing they could do.

And so, he left. Again.

24

VOWS
VERA

Marriage is sacred. And though I managed to hold my head high above the whispers and side comments—that I, a child of God, continued to live in sin with Morris because we were not married—it haunted me. Morris knew. But I never once begged him to put a ring on my finger. I was never the kind to ask anything of a man.

I'd always been independent, ever striving to make ends meet on my own. But the price of that independence was this: men often enjoyed my care and support so much, they saw no reason to make me their wife.

Sun and I had lasted a long time, but those were years I tried to forget. I'd spent weeks of my wages trying to change a man who could not be changed.

My Morris was different—not perfect by any means, but better. We had our differences. Morris had other women from time to time. But he loved me, and I loved him.

Vera

IT WAS ON A SUNDAY EVENING, AS WE ATE DINNER, THAT HE ASKED ME. We usually dined with the radio on, as Morris liked to listen to the news. Then he simply said, "V, cum wi get married."

I was fifty-six years old—a long time for a woman to wait for a proposal from the man she loved. We'd met some fifteen years earlier, and I could hardly believe my ears. But seeing Morris's grin, I knew he meant it.

It took just a few days to get myself ready, and the following week, I became Mrs. Vera Belford. The years had been rocky and hard—Morris had spent time in prison, and he'd been unfaithful, too. But when we wed on that Saturday afternoon in 1978, I was the happiest woman on the island of Jamaica.

Flo's wash belly, Greg, had always spent every spare moment at our house. That morning, as I dressed for my wedding, Greg was there. The boy begged to go to the church, but he couldn't, for this day was meant for adults. I could hardly look after a six-year-old while repeating my vows to the love of my life.

But when we returned for a small dinner reception with friends and family, little Greg was there. Even as I smiled and shared secret jokes with Morris while we sat at the table with a beautifully decorated cake before us, Greg stood in the shadows, watching us without a smile on his face.

As the guests urged us to kiss, and cheers filled our small sitting room, Greg remained silent, ever serious. I saw why he'd been nicknamed "the judge." He hardly liked being around strangers, seldom speaking with those he didn't know. But with family and close friends, he was different—only then could you see his love of books and reading.

I sat there, wondering whether he was jealous or simply angry that he'd missed the ceremony at the church. But when he had a chance, after most of the guests had left, Greg came close, his eyes fixed on the cake—he'd always had a weakness for sweets.

He smiled at us both, for he'd always loved spending time with Morris, too. I knew then that he was happy for me, though, looking at his face and into his eyes, one would never have known little Greg was happy for his granny.

25

GOODBYE GRANNY B
VERA

Caring for a blind mother hadn't been easy. Granny B, my mother, had been bedridden for several years, leaving my sisters and me to share the heavy burden of her care. Since I lived closest, it fell to me to ensure she was cleaned, fed, and tended to daily. I was sixty years old in 1982 when my mother passed away at the age of eighty-two.

The days leading up to the burial were filled with sorrow, but traditions were in place for the dead. Busy nights spent with singing, drinking, and eating—long hours of drunken men arguing, women fussing, and tired children dozing off beneath the trees as the early morning hours crept in. I managed to hold it together through all that, the noise and the distractions. But the day of the funeral, when it was time to say goodbye, I fell apart.

Ma Jane's death had been hard on me, eighteen years earlier. But this was different—Granny B, my mother, was now gone too. She was laid to rest beside Ma Jane and Tata Joe, in the same plot of land where I had been born and raised. The land that had held our family for generations now held another piece of me, another piece of my past. It felt as though I had lost the last connection to my childhood, my roots. The weight of it all pressed on me as the finality of her death sank in.

26

MISS DEL

I could hardly believe Flo's children were all together. Months after Bill's return, once he had adjusted to being with his family, I would visit and still marvel that they were living under the same roof. Flo's seven children were close. They all stayed in a single room in the Longmore house—two big beds for seven siblings. Flo had insisted she wanted her children together.

There was, however, a problem after Bill's return: Miss Del. While it may not have concerned others, Miss Del constantly spoke about the young man's Rastafarian beliefs—and the fact that he hadn't cut his hair. The boy was my grandson, and he was still young. So when I heard the children complain, I made a point of visiting, usually on my way home from the market on Saturdays. The children were always happy to see their granny—sometimes I brought them Anansi Sweetie Bars, their favourite chocolate treat.

I often argued with Miss Del over my grandchildren, mostly because she beat them too much. The woman knew little about loving children and everything about punishing them. She hardly ever spanked Wayne—her favourite. Wayne, Keith's eldest, looked after the younger ones and worked hard, always doing his chores to Miss Del's pleasure. In Miss Del's opinion, Courtney was a little hellion. And to be fair, the boy was a thorn in her side—they didn't like each other. But while she and her brother, Mass Harry, could hardly stand him, Banka adored Courtney. And Courtney knew they didn't like him. So he did things just to aggravate them.

One morning, the children crossed the field between our homes—a field where cows grazed and the children were terrified—but they braved it anyway to take the shortcut to see me. It only took a few minutes to get there—we lived that close. As they told me what Courtney had done the night before, I fell to the floor on my veranda, laughing so hard that tears ran down my cheeks. My grandchildren loved seeing me laugh, and I'm sure Miss Del heard me that morning.

The night before, while the children watched television in the hall, Miss Del and Banka had bid them a pleasant good night. Banka, the children insisted, had nothing to do with what followed—they adored him. The man and his wife were like night and day. After locking themselves in their room, while the children continued watching their show, the entire house went black. Miss Del, having wished them good night, had turned off the main power switch, leaving my grandchildren to stumble through the pitch dark to find their beds.

The younger ones were frightened, and all were disappointed. But Courtney was furious. He told no one his plan. The boy kept himself awake until all was still. Late into the night, while others snored, Courtney crept from bed and made sure Miss Del would pay for what she'd done.

Early the next morning, when the cock crowed and dogs barked, Miss Del rose—as usual, the first to wake. When she flicked the main power switch, there was a loud boom, and the whole house was startled. In the night, Courtney had turned on every appliance in the house. He cranked the TV to full volume, did the same with the stereo, and every other device. When the house erupted in noise, the other children sat up in shock—only Courtney remained calm, grinning from bed.

Later, as they giggled in silence, he boasted of what he'd done—still angry, but proud that he had taught her a lesson. She knew he was the culprit. But for that one time, Miss Del did nothing—though she enjoyed nothing more than flogging that boy.

I laughed all morning. Even after the children left, I laughed again when I told Morris. And seeing him laugh too made me drop to the floor, screaming with laughter.

———

———

———

SEVERAL MONTHS LATER, WHILE SITTING IN MISS MARGARET'S SHOP UP BY Grace Street, I heard a terrible cry from a child. The bawling was so loud it interrupted my conversation. Miss Margaret paused in the middle of weighing out the sugar I was buying and said, "Jesus Christ, ah which pickney dem deh murda?" The sound was awful—like the cry of a doomed hog with its throat slit. I paid it no mind at the time, collected my goods, and headed home.

Minutes later, I walked through my gate and found Greg by the back door. He had come through the shortcut from Miss Del's yard, and he was terrified, weeping uncontrollably. Welts covered his arms and body—marks from Miss Del's strap. The children had told me they were forced to sleep with that long leather belt hanging from the headboard, Miss Del's cure for bed-wetting. They went to bed in fear, and the mornings were even worse if one of them had wet the bed.

But this was during the day—Greg had been at school. This beating wasn't about bed-wetting.

"What happen to you?" I asked. He could barely speak through sobs.

"Miss Del beat mi!" That was obvious. Only her strap could leave welts like that. He explained he'd gotten into a fight with one of Miss Del's adopted boys. She'd recently taken in a pair of brothers, Mickie and Warren. The kids played together often, though Miss Del warned the brothers not to play with Ricky and Greg. But how could you tell children not to play, living under the same roof?

Greg and Warren had a falling out on the walk home. They exchanged blows, as children do, and Warren—after losing—ran home to complain. Instead of talking to them, Miss Del gave Greg a beating he wouldn't forget. I realized it was Greg I'd heard crying at Miss Margaret's shop.

I calmed him, made him sit with me while I cooked supper for Morris and the children. After we ate, I walked Greg home—by the road, not the shortcut.

Miss Del sat on the veranda, poised like the Queen of Sheba. Mass Jakey was there too. The other children loitered in the front yard. When Miss Del saw me, her eyes blinked behind thick bifocals. She said nothing—just waited.

Greg lingered at the gate, afraid to go in.

"Mi deh a Miss Margaret shop and hear Greg bawlin'. Why yuh beat him so?" I asked.

Miss Del grunted. "Greg bright an facety. Who cyan stop mi from beat him?"

We argued, loud enough for all to hear. Neighbours came to their gates. I turned to leave and Greg followed, still wanting to come home with me. I stopped and turned to him. "Gwan back," I said. "Nuh follow me. Ah deh yuh madda an fadda lef unuh."

Miss Del chuckled, mocking us. "Mi nuh know weh him deh run go..."

I turned and stared her down. "Den if mi did want him fi come, him nuh cyan come?"

I knew right then—if I'd told Greg to come, he would have. But he would've paid for it later. So I went home to Morris and the two stepchildren I never wanted. Flo had made her decision years ago—for her children to stay with Miss Del. If only she knew the hell they were living through.

My relationship with Miss Del had always been civil, though I knew she hated me. We had our differences. And I always felt she knew I believed Mass Jakey was too good a man for her.

Shawn was the only girl child in that house. And I always believed she was there only because Miss Del had no choice—she never took in girls. Only boys.

Deleta Longmore (Miss Del)

SHE SAT ON THE VERANDA, HER GAZE FIXED UPON THE WOMAN AS SHE turned toward the gate. Deleta pushed her spectacles back up her nose and grunted, noting that Jakey had remained silent during the entire exchange with Miss Vera. She smiled faintly, noticing that Greg was already walking toward the back of the house—clearly afraid he'd get another flogging if he came too close. Deleta shook her head in disgust, slightly annoyed to see sympathy in Jakey's eyes.

The children loved him, yet they always seemed to sidestep her and cease their playful banter whenever she entered the room. It was no mystery why they adored him—Jakey was gentle, playful, and seldom raised his voice, let alone his hand.

But when Jakey's eyes shifted toward the gate, Deleta felt a sharp twist in her chest. Miss Vera had turned to gaze back into the yard, taking one last protective look at her youngest grandson. The boy was close to his granny and older siblings. And though he didn't misbehave, Greg was too bold in his silence, as far as Deleta was concerned.

The children had all left the front yard, and the neighbours had gone from their front gates, leaving Deleta and her husband seated on the veranda. The way Jakey watched Miss Vera as she walked down the lane made Deleta shift uncomfortably in her chair. She heard Jakey's long sigh—for he had noticed the sudden clench of her fists.

Deleta had kept her suspicions to herself for years. And as God liveth, she knew she was right about it, for she was no fool.

Keith came into her life back when they lived in Balaclava, in 1954 —perfect timing, since Jakey had gone to America to do farm work, and she had needed the distraction more than anything.

The boy arrived as Carl McEwan, but after Deleta's mother had trouble remembering the name, they began calling him Keith Longmore. That was how he became theirs.

She forgot Jakey was sitting beside her, for once again she was plunged into that old chasm of grief.

Jakey sighed again, pulling her back to the present. She glanced at him, the words rising like bile in her throat. She longed to remind him that she had as much claim to Keith's children as Miss Vera did. She wanted to shout that she was the one who raised that boy until he became a man.

And more than anything else, she wanted Jakey to remember what Keith had meant to them when he came into their lives.

She hadn't carried Keith in her womb, not for one minute. But in her heart, he was her son.

And after all these years—after all she'd done for Keith and his children—it was Miss Vera they called Granny. It was Miss Vera who got the real smiles.

To the very children she had fed and raised, she was just Miss Del. *Imagine.*

Jacob Longmore (Banka)

JACOB HAD ALWAYS LIVED BY THE MANTRA THAT IF ONE DIDN'T HAVE something sensible to say, one should say nothing. Miss Vera had stopped to chat with someone on the road, so she was still in view— and as much as he tried to avert his gaze, Jacob found it near impossible.

Sitting beneath his wife's scrutiny, he sighed, unsure whether it was guilt or the quiet fury radiating from Deleta that made him feel so unsettled.

His thoughts drifted to that Sunday afternoon in 1944, when he married Deleta—the woman he called D—in Auchtembeddie, Manchester. Her brother, Harold Sanchez, had served as witness. Mass Harry, as everyone in the district called him, would later move to Clark's Town to live with them. Even now, Jacob could hear the rhythmic pounding from Harry's little shop to the right of the house— he was a shoemaker and seldom idle.

Their wedding had been a simple affair. Jacob was thirty and working as a baker; Deleta, a seamstress, was twenty-seven. It had been the right time. She already had a young son, Elbert, who was four at the time. Jacob took them both in and loved them as his own.

After some years, the family moved to Clark's Town. Jacob had accepted a short-term job opening a bakery for Oswald Chin. What was supposed to be six months became a permanent move. He sent for his family, and Deleta began a new career as a teacher. They settled first in Bottom Town. During the week, Deleta worked in Kinloss and came home on weekends, while Jacob ran the bakery and looked after the household.

But beneath the quiet routines of their life, sorrow lived like a shadow. Jacob's thoughts returned to Lucas—their son. Born in 1940, Lucas had been just fourteen when a truck struck him and ended his life. Jacob had only been in America for two weeks when it happened. The news had shattered him, but he stayed to finish the six-month contract.

Two months after Lucas's death, Keith entered their lives.

The boy had arrived as Carl McEwan, but when Deleta's mother had trouble with the name, they started calling him Keith Longmore.

Jacob had met him upon returning to Jamaica and saw immediately how Deleta clung to the boy with a mother's hunger. She'd poured her grief into Keith, and Jacob too had taken him in—he needed to. Keith became the balm for a wound that refused to close. To Deleta, he was a second chance. To Jacob, he was the pride of a father who'd lost his only son.

Jacob stirred from the memory and glanced at his wife again. Her silence grated, but he knew better than to start a quarrel he'd never win.

His affair with Vera had begun in the early 1960s. It hadn't lasted long, and they'd been discreet—but Jacob was certain Deleta had known. Over the years, the two women had done their best to remain civil—for the sake of the grandchildren, if nothing else.

But Jacob had long suspected that their uneasy truce masked a deeper, older wound.

So, as he'd done for many years, Jacob sat on the veranda in the shadow of his wife's anger and said nothing.

Vera

AFTER FLO DECIDED IT WAS BEST FOR HER CHILDREN TO RESIDE WITH THE Longmores, I was angry. I felt slighted—furious, even—that she wanted those kids to stay with Keith's guardian. My life with Morris was far from perfect; we had our own share of troubles. But those children were my own flesh and blood, and the fact that Miss Del had spent those years gloating infuriated me. Eventually, though, my anger gave way to concern—for Flo's children, not myself.

The siblings usually came to me as a group with their complaints. They were close, bound together despite their differences—which were normal for children growing up in tight quarters. Courtney and Wayne were always fighting, and although Courtney was foul-mouthed and full of threats, he was always bested by his older brother. Bill, being the newest addition—none of the others had known of him before he came—had to adjust to being the eldest. It took time. I wasn't just their pleasant granny; I was often a referee. Many of their conflicts spilled into my kitchen or played out on my veranda.

I reminded them of their roots.

"Unuh come from one madda," I'd say to them. "One madda! So unuh nuh need fi fight lakka puss an dog."

Each of them was different.

The wash belly, Greg, was quiet, creative, and always deep in imagination. Ricky, by contrast, was always out pretending to be a soldier or warrior, always coming home to Miss Del with cuts, scrapes, and bruises. Greg returned from school neat as a pin, looking just as he had in the morning. Ricky's uniform, though—ripped, dusty, covered in burrs. Greg kept his shirt buttoned to the neck; Baboo, as Banka called Ricky, looked like he'd wrestled a goat. Still, the two youngest were close, often dressed like twins.

Wayne was orderly, something of a disciplinarian, and the younger ones usually listened to him. Garth had a bright, outgoing personality. Shawn, ever moody, was a tomboy. Bill had a quiet pain about him. He caged his emotions, and I saw it in his eyes—especially when he spoke of Miss Del's disapproval. Courtney was the prankster, the mischief-maker. He did the strangest things. Once, during one of their rainy-day *"church"* sessions in the house, he played the parson and dipped scotch bonnet peppers into the holy water while the others prayed with their eyes shut. That communion Courtney served to his siblings made them choke and cough from the hot peppers. I heard these stories from the wash belly whenever he visited, and I couldn't help but laugh.

But my concern grew for Flo's only daughter.

Most mornings, when I took the shortcut path to Miss Del's yard to surprise my grandchildren, I'd find a sullen Shawn standing beneath the breadfruit tree at the washstand. I never had to ask why she looked so down. There, before Erica, in a basin of soap and water, were Miss Del's silken drawers. It was Shawn's duty to wash Miss Del's panties.

There was something in that child's eyes—something angry and raw, something that even hatred hadn't yet managed to blot out.

There was nothing I could do to help her. She was in Miss Del's house, under Miss Del's rules.

Every morning, it was also Shawn's job to empty Miss Del's chamberpot. Not the usual plastic kind, but a massive white enamel pail—high enough so Miss Del wouldn't have to squat too low in the night. I'd pass through early and see the rancid look on my granddaughter's face as she lugged that pail by its handle to the latrine. Miss Del never brought it out herself. Shawn had to collect it first thing every morning.

I hated the condition. But it was all out of my hands.

My grandchildren weren't in my care.

27

LELA AND MORRIS
VERA

I busied myself with checking on my grandchildren, looking after Morris's household, and tending to his children. Peggy was old enough now to spend more time with her mother, but Junior—though he visited her from time to time—hardly wanted to leave his father's house. The boy lingered on, always a thorn in my side, almost willing me to hate him. Over the years we managed to mend our relationship, but those truces rarely lasted more than a few months or a year. Junior was much older than Greg by several years, but the two did spend time together in Morris's workshop.

Morris earned a decent living from his carpentry—he made good furniture, was often commissioned to craft coffins for the dead, and even built houses. Greg and Junior would stay in the workshop for hours, near the front of the property, while I stayed busy in the kitchen or tended to things around the house. I saw the joy in Morris's eyes during the months when his son and I were on good terms; it brought peace to the household.

One Sunday, after Morris and I had argued, I made the mistake of saying some terrible things. Though we were married, his appetite for other women had never dulled. I'd heard the rumours—and had even proved them true—that he'd been unfaithful again. I hadn't gone to church that morning. After I confronted him, he grew so angry I feared he might strike me. He never did, but that day I left the house and called my sister.

"Lela," I said, "Morris frighten mi... gwaan like im a-go lik mi." I told her about the other woman, and Lela became furious. When the line went dead, I rushed home, anxious, certain she was already on her way to the house. I hurried to make things right with Morris, for everything had to look right when Lela arrived. I hadn't forgotten what she'd done to Wilfred when Flo was a child, and I couldn't bear the thought of her holding my husband to the ground and forcing me to beat him. Morris was a strong man, but I doubted he could manage my sister.

Lela arrived at my gate and called aloud, her voice rising above the bark of the dogs. The sun was hot, the ground dry, and she had come all the way from Clark's Town to Hyde on foot in that heat. I'd just fixed Morris's lunch and rushed through the hall. "Dat sound like Lela," he said as I passed.

I met her at the gate, and before unlatching it, I begged her to stay calm. "Lela, duh, nuh badda seh nuttin to Morris..."

I led her into the kitchen, where Morris sat eating. I saw the rage on Lela's face—the clenched fists, the wide-legged stance like she was ready to pounce. My heart slammed against my ribs. I felt sure Morris knew I had told her. He sat calmly, sipping the cold drink I'd given him, ankles crossed beneath the table. I reminded myself they'd always gotten on well. *Nuttin nah guh happen*, I thought. Or maybe I just willed it so.

Then Lela said, after a long breath, "Afternoon, Morris."

Morris uncrossed his ankles. He grinned and wiped juice from his lips with the back of his hand. "Aright, Miss Lela." I exhaled.

The conversation drifted from one topic to the next. Lela loved to talk politics, and since Morris always kept up with the news, there was plenty to discuss. Later that Sunday, as she left, Morris gave her a bag of fresh produce and sugar cane he'd harvested himself. He even sent some of his tobacco for my cousin Lucille, who—like Ma Jane—always loved to smoke.

That night, I lay in bed relieved that my sister had decided to hold her tongue. I was certain things would have escalated if she'd said even one word about my quarrel with Morris. But Lela never understood that Morris was different from the rest. For all our conflicts, he never raised a hand to me. And he always promised he would never leave.

Vera

UNLIKE MANY OTHERS, I UNDERSTOOD MY HUSBAND—FOR IT WAS I WHO had waited for him after he was imprisoned for chopping that man. It was I who visited him during those long months, I who married him in spite of the gossip and his many faults. Morris would only eat the food I prepared, for I was the only one he trusted. And why should he trust any other woman?

He always spoke of that one woman who had stooped over his food, and ever since, Morris had grown superstitious, seeing evil in every strange thing. One evening, as we sat on the veranda with a few of the grandchildren visiting, Morris was perched on the bench beside the ledge. A fly landed on the rim of his glass. My superstitious husband grinned, pointing to the fly, then motioning toward the children.

"Rock-stone mouth!"

That was Morris's famous alternative to cussing—he knew how much I hated to hear him curse. Not that it ever stopped him when he was angry. The fly crawled downward into his nearly empty glass.

"Yuh si dat?" he said, nodding toward the children. Greg was staring at him with wide-eyed belief. "Dem send im come fi hear wah wi deh seh..."

The older grandchildren chuckled behind Morris's back, but the younger ones believed him—that some wicked person had truly sent the fly to spy on us.

I admit, I've always been a little superstitious, but even I couldn't agree with Morris about the flies. Not that I ever dared say so. Yet, over time, his habits became my own. I found myself using his famous phrase whenever I felt the urge to curse.

And as we grew older together, I began to believe—just a little— that maybe those cursed flies were listening in on our private talks. So every night, we shut the doors and windows. Not just to keep out the mosquitoes—but to keep out the nosey flies.

28

LESTER WALLACE
VERA

In spite of our conflicts, Morris and I shared a strong bond as man and wife. Though he never confessed to his dalliances, I wasn't a fool. Still, unlike my past relationships, I refused to let him go— for I was already in my fifties when we married. But my love for Morris was everlasting. I loved him from the first day I laid eyes on him.

It was early in the evening. We had just finished supper and were sitting on the veranda. The view before us was a pleasant one—the mountains in the distance clear against the fading sky. The breeze was cool and soft, the kind that made the evening feel peaceful.

We sat close together on benches Morris had built himself, and just after we finished singing a hymn, we heard footsteps coming from the side of the house. I knew right away who it was—Flo's wash belly.

Greg came around to the front steps of the veranda with a smile. "Eveling, Mass Morris...eveling, Granny." As usual, he smiled without showing his little white teeth. He was only seven, quiet by nature, and often played alone except when with friends or his brother, Ricky. Flo's two youngest were close, born just over a year apart.

All my grandchildren visited often, but for Greg, my house was a second home. Miss Del didn't like this much, but the boy was happiest in my company or among his six siblings. And he was spoiled, too—wash bellies usually are.

Greg stayed until it got dark. The three of us sat on the veranda watching the stars. A little later, Junior joined us. He stood quietly by the steps, not saying a word. Morris's son was a tall, lean teenager—fearless, but it was his father who kept him in check, made sure he never disrespected me.

Junior and I had our moments. Sometimes we were the best of friends, sitting together, chatting and laughing, never knowing how long our truce would last.

Peenie wallies flickered in the dark, and dogs barked in the distance. I'd already sent Junior to tell Miss Del that Greg would be staying the night, so we lingered outside, chewing on sugar cane Morris had grown himself.

That night, the four of us shared something rare—peace. I saw the joy in Morris's eyes, saw how pleased he was that his son and I were getting along.

The next morning, Morris left early for work. Junior and Greg stayed around the yard while I did the washing. Around midday, I took a rest and sat with the boys on the veranda. That's when we saw Morris returning through the gate. He wasn't alone.

He pushed the gate inward, his face drawn and solemn. Behind him was a man I recognized—a post office worker. He delivered telegrams.

My heart sank.

Morris came straight to my side, leaving the man to speak.

"Miss Vera," the man said. "Mi come fi tell yuh seh—"

"Whaap'm?" I placed my hand over my chest, already fearing the worst. My mind flew to Flo, all the way in Canada.

"Is yuh bredda, Miss Vera… Lester…"

"V…" Morris's hand settled gently on my shoulder.

"Miss Vera—"

"Im dead! Im dead!" I screamed.

I hadn't seen Lester in years. But we wrote often, and now and then he'd send me a few pounds from England. I missed him so—my favourite brother, my heart. Our father, Richard Wallace, had many children, but Lester and I had been close since we were small.

I didn't need to hear the rest. I didn't want to hear that man read the telegram. I already knew.

I wept uncontrollably. My cries echoed up the lane and into every home, for I had lost a part of me.

My brother, Lester Wallace, was dead.

29

CHANGES
VERA

It was the 1980s, and the world was changing. Flo had been gone for what seemed like an eternity, for her youngest child had just turned eight. I missed my daughter dearly—she was half of me, my one child. I was fifty-eight years old, but I still looked young, for I hadn't a single grey hair upon my head. And though I was a married woman, I still turned the heads of men, old and young alike. But I was a happy wife. I had struggled for many years, wondering why it had been so difficult to find a man, for my sisters had all found love early. I eventually found Morris—the love of my life.

Tutu Barrett had loved me, and I loved him, too, for I believed it took love for me to conceive. From Tutu Barrett, I got my one child. But the love I found with Morris was something different.

I remembered the days when I hummed and danced to the popular songs of my time, when the music and cheers of others pushed me toward the centre of the dance floor and upon the stage. But I'd been so young then. In my later years, I heard songs on the radio that had little meaning to me, songs such as *Another One Bites the Dust*. How could anyone dance to such music? But as I said earlier, the world as I knew it was changing. And in that same year, Keith and Flo made their very first move.

Shawn, their only girl, was sent to Montego Bay to live with Lela's daughter, Claudia—or Dawn, as we all called her—while attending Herbert Morrison school.

When news came that I would have my very first great-grandchild, I was in shock. Courtney was just a boy of sixteen when the girl had the child. The girl was known as Mushie, daughter of Morris's good friend, Mass Cooley. Miss Del had been enraged, but I couldn't be angry with the boy over what had already happened. Courtney's child was named Shara McEwan.

Miss Del and I had our differences; however, my daughter's children had been left in our care. With news of Bill's association with bad company—some young man from St. Mary—we made certain Keith and Flo knew their eldest was headed down the wrong path. Those were days when the young hardly listened to those left in charge of them. Wayne had started to have his own way too—it had become difficult to control these young men as they matured. They'd begun staying out late, even sleeping out at night. At that age, Miss Del's threats to lock them out at night brought little or no deterrence.

My grandsons were by no means terrible—just easily led astray, and neither I nor Miss Del wanted that for them.

My daughter and her husband made arrangements to begin moving their family to Toronto, Canada. It was then I met the leader of Flo's church in Toronto—for it was he who brought Bill to Canada. So much had changed over the years. It was impossible for Keith or Flo to return to Jamaica, as they would never have been allowed back into Canada.

Wayne moved to Canada just a few months after his older brother, but he travelled alone and was hardly given a chance to prepare. Wayne was at my house cooking one afternoon when Lela arrived for him. The less they knew, we thought, the better—it would lessen the chance of loose tongues. They all had friends, and would no doubt mention they were going away. That day, Lela arrived at my house and simply told Wayne he was to go to Miss Del's house and gather what clothes he could. They left for Montego Bay that very evening, where the boy stayed with my niece, Claudia. Wayne left for Toronto the following day.

It was easy for one to travel to Canada back then. In July of 1982, Courtney and Shawn traveled to Toronto—their first summer vacation abroad. Shawn, who was maturing into a shapely young woman at age twelve, returned with what those abroad called a Walkman. I'd never seen or heard of such a thing before—a tiny radio with wired head-phones and puffy orange sponges over the ears. When Shawn placed the thing over my ears, I was instantly in my own world and talked so loudly with the music playing. And again, I heard another of those songs that meant nothing to me, something about a tiger's eye—or was it the eye of a tiger? I really can't recall.

But my son-in-law, Keith, was a clever man. When I spoke with him from the only public payphone in Clark's Town, he and Flo explained their plan and why it was imperative all the children leave Jamaica as soon as possible. Keith had read in the Toronto papers that changes were coming—soon visitors would no longer be allowed into Canada without a visa.

During the weeks leading up to July 1983, I warned Ricky and Greg not to utter a word of the plan to their friends, for I was a superstitious woman, and people were capable of envy and wickedness. I'd not forgotten what was done to Flo when she became pregnant with Bill. All the plans had been made—the letter written by their school princi-pal, Miss Reid; the passports ordered and in hand. Flo's bishop would travel with the boys, who were just eleven and ten years old.

I saw them the night before they left in July, but early the next morning, as they prepared to leave Miss Del's house, I couldn't stay away. It was still dark when I got to the house. I wept to see them go, for I had no idea when I would see them again. My two youngest grand-children left for Kingston that morning with Courtney and Flo's closest friend, Gloria—the children and many others called her Auntie Pet. I watched them walk away from Miss Del's house with one tiny suitcase containing all their good clothes. Four of Flo's children were gone from me. Only three were left.

Courtney, Shawn, and Garth left the following week with a family friend, Chris—the mother of Miss Del's grandchildren. I was there the day the last of my grandchildren went away. In Courtney's eyes, I saw such eagerness for a new adventure—a new life. Garth, always pleasant, was smiling as he prepared to go. At nearly sixteen, he was ready for change. Shawn was excited, too, but I saw she was especially pleased to escape the chores Miss Del had forced upon her, simply because she was a girl.

The children embraced Banka lovingly. It was evident they would miss him dearly. I sometimes wonder how Miss Del and her husband were ever matched, for they were so different. Miss Del seldom demonstrated affection, and that day she stood boldly, flat-footed, showing no sign of sorrow. She accepted Courtney's embrace in silence, grunted with a smile as Garth said goodbye, but it was only Shawn she had words for.

Miss Del's large eyes bulged behind the fogged lenses of her spectacles, and they seemed to scrutinize the young girl. "All yuh," Miss Del said, "mi nah expect fi hear fram yuh." Shawn said nothing, and she didn't embrace the woman whose panties she'd washed every morning since she was old enough to learn how.

Miss Del shrugged knowingly, for it was evident she didn't expect a goodbye embrace from the girl.

By the end of July, I found myself alone, without visits from my seven grandchildren. And although I still had Morris with me, it was never the same. Still, I was proud—happy even—that Keith and Flo had managed to unite their family after so many years.

———————

———————

———————

Vera

THE MONTHS PASSED QUICKLY, AND AFTER YEARS OF COMMUNICATING with my grandchildren through letters and telephone calls, I began to wonder if I would ever see them again. But by 1985, things had changed for the better in Canada. The children were settled, and their mother had been granted permission to travel. Flo came home. She was forty-two years old; I was sixty-three. It had been ten long years since I'd last seen my child. She was beautiful. My daughter looked the same in my eyes, and as for myself, I knew she saw the same woman. Seeing Flo again was the best thing that had happened to me in years. I saw photos of my grandchildren and was in shock—they had grown so much since they left.

Two years later, in the month of December, Flo returned to Jamaica again. Auntie Pet's mother, Mrs. Rubina Allen—known to all as Mother Allen—had died. I visited the house myself during the nights they sang old songs, ate various foods, and drank strong drinks. Bredda Nattie, now an old man of ninety-one, was still strong, for he would live well past his one-hundredth year.

Flo arrived two weeks before a big surprise. And after the funeral, her wash-belly—little Greg—came home. But Greg was no longer little. He was fourteen and tall. When he spoke, it felt as if the ground rumbled. I wept at the sight of him, but I had to ask how such a deep voice came from a wiry young man like him. At first glance, I mistook him for his brother, Courtney, for like his brother, Greg had their father's eyes—only slightly bigger.

That morning, right there in my kitchen, I embraced my last grand-son. I also embraced the stranger with him—a white girl they called Carrie. She must have been nineteen years old and had eyes that seemed to change like one of the cats I kept around the house. I couldn't tell what colour those eyes were. But Carrie was cheerful. She was Courtney's girlfriend, and it was clear the family loved her. She and Greg were inseparable.

Flo, Carrie, and Greg all slept in the same bed when they stayed at my house, for there was only one spare room. And each morning, I would weaken with laughter, for Carrie was afraid of every insect in the house.

"Granny!" Even Carrie called me this. "Luk, Granny...luk pon di big cockroach!"

Carrie was a white girl with eyes like Ma Jane's, but she had learned to speak like us. With your eyes closed, you'd never have guessed she wasn't from Jamaica. I buckled with laughter until tears flowed from my eyes.

Even Junior, Morris's son, was in awe of her. I overheard him out on the veranda, speaking with her.

"Mi neva talk to a white sumady before." he said.

I realized how true that was, for Junior was quiet and withdrawn—a man who'd spent much of his life a loner.

Flo and I became concerned each morning, for Carrie had been complaining of nausea and had started having nosebleeds. She would stand there in my kitchen, a tissue pressed to her nose and her head tilted back. She never noticed a thing, while Flo and I exchanged knowing glances.

30

GONE AH 'FARIN'
VERA

It took some time to acquire it, but eventually Flo succeeded in getting a visa for my first visit abroad. My daughter had visited Jamaica several times and had tried so hard to get me a visa; however, her efforts were unsuccessful. Still, Flo never gave up. She returned to Canada after telling off the immigration officer in Kingston. Then she met with her Member of Parliament in Canada, and the next time she came back to Kingston, the visa was granted.

I left for Canada in the summer of 1988, knowing I would miss Morris dearly. But the time had come to visit another country, for Morris had already been abroad. He held me the night before my trip and teased me, ever laughing.

"V, yuh deh guh ah farin," he grinned, so wide I could see all the gaps in his mouth, for he'd lost several teeth.

"V, yuh mek sure everybody nuh stay pon one side ah di plane... di plane a-go tilt..."

I playfully slapped him for being so silly. "Morris!"

I left Clark's Town that day wearing one of my best wigs. I was terrified the entire journey to the airport. After I wept and bid Morris good-bye, I boarded the aircraft, wondering how I would survive several hours in such a small space. I was suddenly brought back to my childhood, for I could hardly endure being in a car with the windows shut. But I prayed all the way. As the aircraft descended, I saw thousands of lights—colourful, beautiful, and bright.

How I managed to contain the joy I felt, I do not know, for seeing Keith and Flo with their family in Canada was unbelievable. Bill, who'd been taken from us just as he was beginning to speak his first words, was now a grown man. And Carrie—who had once walked the old floors of my kitchen back in Jamaica—I found very huge with Courtney's child. I smiled, for I had known the girl was pregnant several months before, when she woke each morning feeling nauseous and sick.

Later that year, Carrie gave birth to a son. And just a month later, Garth had his first son too—two great-grandchildren, only a month apart.

31

THE LONGMORES
VERA

It seemed my best black dress was only ever worn at funerals. I donned that dress twice in one year—June and October of 1991—for that was the year Miss Del and Mass Jakey died.

Mr. Longmore had been ill for some time, and when the end was near, it seemed Miss Del fell into a deep depression. He had been so dear to her. After Mass Jakey passed, Flo, Keith, and several of the children came for the funeral. But the wife he left behind never recovered. She was heartbroken, and she was ill.

Keith and Flo returned to Jamaica just months later, as Miss Del's health declined. When I went to visit her at home, just days before she was taken to the hospital, I knew she would die. I saw it in her eyes—there was no will left to live. In the presence of my daughter, she even told her adopted son, Keith, that she couldn't go on.

Jacob Longmore had been her life. So it made sense, when she lay on that hospital bed, her voice weak but her glare still sharp, that she whispered her truth.

"Mi nah guh live without Jakey," she said.

That's what she always called him—Jakey, short for Jacob. Mass Jakey simply called her "D."

And so it was that Miss Del died just four months after she lost her husband. They were buried side-by-side on the same land they had shared for many years—the same land where my grandchildren had grown up.

On both occasions, I stood by their graves, looking into the dark, dusty chasm of the earth. I was saved by God's grace, baptized, and Holy Ghost-filled. But even so, I couldn't fully come to terms with the truth: that to relinquish my youth, and eventually the very breath I breathed, was inevitable.

I believed the Word—that it is appointed to us all once to die, then the judgment shall come. But as I watched Miss Del's coffin disappear into the ground and dirt tossed over it, I found myself wishing I could live forever.

But Ma Jane had always said, even when I was young:

"Once a man, twice a child..."

And then we die.

I went home to Morris that night after the burial, hardly in the mood to speak, troubled in my spirit. The days, the months, the years —they had grown so short, it felt as if time itself had skipped ahead. My mind was consumed by one thought: that sooner or later, we would all be gone...

32

VIRGIE
VERA

There were several other visits to Canada over the years. And although I loved being with my family, I detested the cold weather. More than anything else, I missed my Morris.

At first, I couldn't imagine how anyone could endure such freezing temperatures for so many months. My second visit was a long one—I had spent several months in Canada. When I returned home, Morris teased me.

"V, yuh tun farina now..."

I smiled at him, for he was grinning like a little boy, showing off those toothless gaps.

I returned to Canada again in September of 1992—and it turned out to be the worst trip of my life.

It had only been a week since I arrived. Flo and Greg had gone out to a wedding that Saturday, but I wasn't alone. That house was always full. I'd been downstairs in the basement watching television—most of the shows kept me entertained. Flo and Greg had just come back home. Greg went upstairs to change while Flo and I sat and chatted about the wedding.

Then the telephone rang.

I wasn't paying attention to what she was saying—not until I heard the gasp.

"What? Who?"

Flo sprang from the chair, and I looked at her. I'd heard my sister's name.

After she hung up, Flo turned to me, her face pale, her eyes wide.

"Mama..."

"Flo, whaap'm?" Her eyes filled with tears. "Flo! Whaap'm to Virgie?"

And when she told me, I could do nothing but scream. I couldn't walk.

I can't explain how I made it up those stairs. My voice echoed inside my head as I crawled across the basement floor and pulled myself up, step by step. By the time I reached the second floor I was exhausted, but I kept going, crawling like a child, groaning and screaming louder.

I felt the grief grab hold of me—my heart, my soul. As I dragged myself up toward the third floor, I screamed my grandson's name.

"Greg! Greg! Lawd Jesus! Greg!"

He met me at the top of the stairs, eyes wide, half-dressed.

"Granny, whaap'm?"

He looked terrified. His mouth hung open—it was clear he thought something had happened to his mother.

"Granny, what's wrong?"

I could hardly speak. I was still crawling. I reached for his feet and held them as I wept.

"Dem... Virgie... dead!"

Greg blinked at me, confused.

"Granny, what? Aunt Virgie? Whaap'm?"

"Dem kill Virgie," I said.

"What?"

"Dem... dem..."

I inched closer, summoning what little strength I had left.

"Dem cut har throat!"

I rolled over onto my back and wailed.

My sister, Virginia, was dead.

I was on a flight back to Jamaica just a few days later. I wasn't going to miss my sister's funeral. I left Flo's home early that morning, still weeping.

Virgie was seventy-five years old. A shopkeeper. She had worked so hard over the years. Though her husband had passed and her son had begged her to leave the small village of Hague, she refused. She was independent. She wanted to stay in her home, to run her little shop. She'd lived there so many years.

Masked robbers had broken into her house to steal from her. She fought them—four young men. And they slit her throat for the money she had inside.

Flo and Greg came to Jamaica the following year for Virgie's memorial service. I could hardly bear it. It felt like I had just lost her.

I still grieve her now.

She was dear to me.

My sister.

33

MI NAME VERA BELFORD

VERA

I visited Canada for the last time at the age of seventy-six, and it was the longest of my visits. I stayed with Flo and her family for over a year.

Flo has always been my child, and I her mother, but since we were both raised by Ma Jane, we lived like sisters. I smile at the thought that I, the mother, had begun referring to my daughter as *Mammy*. Flo's children always called her Mommy, and Keith, Daddy.

So when Mammy called me one evening from Canada, bringing me up to speed on all that had been happening with the family, I was pleased to hear things were well. Shawn had since been married, and two years earlier, she'd had a son.

When Flo was finished talking, she put Keith on the phone.

"Granny!" he said. That's what he always called me now—no longer Miss Vera, for I'd become a mother to my daughter's husband, and he had become my child.

Keith treated me with such care, and showed such love, and I deeply regretted ever doubting him all those years ago. He loved my child and had only ever been good to her. And though I had once questioned whether he was the right one for her, Keith had never thrown that back at me. If he held any ill feelings, I never saw them in him.

"Eveling, Daddy...how yuh duh?"

"Mi aright, Granny. Missah Morris aright?"

"Yes, Daddy. Im cum in fram grung and deh baide, Daddy."

I heard Keith pause and sniff before answering—he'd always suffered from sinusitis.

"Granny, listen mi..." He sniffed again. "Flo seh shi want yuh cum back ah Canada."

My heart raced with sudden excitement. I had always loved those visits abroad. But I also knew how Morris would feel about me leaving again. He never complained, but I knew how much he missed me—after all, it was I who cooked his meals, washed his clothes, kept the house clean, and warmed his bed at night.

"Aright, Daddy," I said. "Mi wi talk wid Morris."

We said our goodbyes, and I hung up the phone, my whole body charged with sudden joy. Morris had already eaten his dinner and was just finishing his bath. I began to prepare myself to deliver the news, for Daddy wanted me to leave for Canada the following week.

Vera

AFTER SEVERAL MONTHS OF LIVING IN CANADA, FLO DECIDED IT WAS BEST I remained there. She had plans to sponsor me. Becoming a permanent resident in a foreign country had never been on my mind—I would never have wanted to leave Morris behind. But Flo explained that I could live in Canada for a while and then sponsor Morris, my husband.

I doubted very much that Morris would want to leave Jamaica to live abroad. Still, I promised to try. I loved the warm months but despised the winter. Whenever I stepped outside in the cold, my entire body shivered. I remember slipping on the ice one Sunday after church and falling right on my backside in Flo's driveway. It was freezing—I could hardly feel my face as the wind tore at my skin. My shoes skidded, and I landed flat on my back with my feet in the air. I couldn't move until Greg came out and helped me up off the ice. And I was certain I saw the little bugger grinning, though he tried his best not to laugh at his granny.

I missed Morris so much that I sometimes felt the need to return home. I worried over him at night—wondering if he'd eaten well before bed, how he was managing with the laundry, the cooking, the cleaning. Those had been my duties for so many years.

When a letter arrived from a good friend in Jamaica, I read it several times—and I was devastated. Morris had been messing around with another woman.

Flo was furious when I said I had to leave.

"Mama, yuh a-go mess up di whole business," she told me.

But I was adamant. I needed to go home... needed to save my marriage. Morris needed me, and I had to go.

Keith and Flo finally conceded. I returned to Jamaica—and I never went back to Canada again.

When I got home, I sought out the woman who had the audacity to go after my husband. I confronted her out on the street. I can't explain what came over me—why I felt like I wanted to fight this woman. I was in my late seventies, and I would've been no match for her. Morris was in his late sixties, and this dutty gal—as I called her—was much younger.

Flo eventually heard about the confrontation—only God knows who told her. She called and said it was a disgrace, an old woman like me quarrelling out in the street over a man. But Morris was my husband. I didn't deny wanting to fight for him, but I stayed silent on the phone and listened to my daughter's admonitions. And all the while, I wondered what she would've done if another woman had tried to take Keith from her. But I dared not say it.

Several years passed. By the time I was in my early eighties, I was constantly complaining to Flo and Keith about Morris. I was convinced the man was against me. We quarrelled nearly every day—more than we ever did when we were young. I'd see him sneaking away beyond the fence to visit another woman, a neighbour he'd taken a liking to.

I begged Flo to come for me, to take me back to Canada. I couldn't endure it anymore. My hair had gone grey. My back hurt so bad I had to walk bent at the waist.

When Greg visited Jamaica in 2005, I begged him to talk to Mammy and Daddy, to ask them to send for me so I could leave again. Morris was out that day, and Greg stood in my dining room while I poured my heart out.

"Granny, I don't understand," he said. "Why can't you and Mass Morris get along?"

My hearing had started to fail, and Greg had never been one to speak loudly.

"Wah?" I said, turning my good ear. "Mi cyan hear suh gud, Greg. Wah yuh seh?"

He moved closer, arms folded. "Granny, mi seh...wah mek yuh an Mass Morris cyan get along?"

"Greg," I sighed. "Di man wicked."

"But he's your husband, Granny." He gave me a look—half stern, half amused.

I told him what Morris had done.

"Greg, mi cyan tek ih." I wiped at my tears. "Ih betta mi stay ah Canada..."

I looked down at my hands in my lap, shaking my head. "Mi cyan tek ih. Morris grab di machete and cum up inna mi face and him seh, 'Yuh...ah gwine kill yuh!'"

Greg's eyes widened. "Granny, mi nuh believe dat... mi cyan believe that." He slipped his hands into his pockets, quiet now.

I took the chance to tell him about the other woman.

"Greg, yuh thirty-three years old—mi last grandson. And mi eighty-three, so mi can tell yuh dis..." I paused. "Di other night, mi inna mi bed deh sleep, and mi wake up fe ketch Morris deh pull open mi legs."

Greg's mouth fell open before he dropped his head in laughter.

"But Granny," he said, "he's your husband... and if he wants to have—"

I cut him off, waving my hands. "Greg, mi tell Morris seh mi nuh duh dem sumting deh again."

He shrugged. "Then why yuh worrying 'bout him going to the other woman's house if yuh nah give him what he want? Mek him duh wah him waan duh wid di woman..."

Flo's wash belly had a point.

But I was a jealous woman. How could I sit in that house and cook Morris's food while he jumped the fence to go across the field and lay with another woman? I was his wife—not her. I was the one who had his name and wore his ring—not the other woman.

I was Vera Belford.

Vera

MY GRANDSON, GREG, WAITED WITH ME UNTIL MORRIS ARRIVED THAT day, and I was certain the two would be happy to see each other—for Greg had spent many of his young days in our home. He was so tiny back then, Flo's little wash belly. Morris would come home after working all day and sit at the table to eat, and Greg always sat beneath that dining table, playing. Eventually, he'd end up tugging at Morris's feet, for Morris never wore shoes on the floors I'd kept spotless. Greg would sit beneath the table and tug on Morris's long, slender toes.

And there he was that day, so many years later, standing in the same house, near that same dining table—a grown man now, tall and slender, all ready to admonish me.

I had told Greg how Morris had been treating me. I'd even explained how Morris's son, Junior, hated me so. But Greg already knew. He'd seen it himself when he was just a boy—how rude that child had been toward me. We sat in the hall as I told my grandson how I feared for my life. I spoke of the threatening gazes, the contempt, and Junior's intent to set Morris against me. And it had been working, too. I was certain the two of them were conspiring in my own home.

"Granny," Greg said, "I'm going to talk with Junior."

"No! Greg!" I stretched out my arms, palms wide open as I begged him not to approach Junior. "Im a-go kill mi!"

"Granny, I'm just gonna say hi, that's all." Greg was already heading for the door, and I felt my heart leap from my chest and lodge itself in my throat. I took a deep breath.

"Greg, nuh seh anything...im wi kill mi..." I could see it in those big eyes—he didn't believe me.

Greg went around to the back of the house, where Junior's quarters were, and I tried to busy myself with whatever I could find—anything to calm myself...

34

CLEMENT BELFORD (JUNIOR)
CLEMENT

I was seated in my little room going over plans for some chairs I was about to make—because like my father, I'm a carpenter. I heard the deep rumble of someone's voice and knew Greg had come to see Miss Vera. I stayed where I was. Greg always came around to see me at some point.

After a while, he was at my door, wearing his usual smile. We shook hands.

"Hey Junior, what's up?" he asked. It was always strange to see how big Greg had gotten.

"Bwoy, Greg, everyting aright, still." I smiled, still a bit in disbelief that Miss Vera's little grandson was now a full-grown man. "Mi jus ah gwaan, yuh know…"

Greg paused before getting to the real reason he'd come around.

"Junior, I kinda know you and Granny never really got along…I remember. But how come you guys can't get along after all these years?"

Leaning against the doorframe, I shook my head, eyes fixed on the floor.

"Miss Vera cyan like mi," I said. "Shi always try fi start up some argument or di oddah."

Greg stepped in a little closer, hands still in his pockets. "What shi duh?" he asked.

I shrugged. "Miss Vera always hab grievance wid mi, Greg...ah dat mi ah tell yuh." He stood quiet, just listening. "Di oddah day—bout few months back—Miss Vera did ah cook some peas soup. An afta she wash di peas, she dash weh di wata out di winda. Couple ah di peas drop 'pon di side ah di kitchen wall, and soon some shoot start grow. Likkle while afta dat, di shoot dem bear peas. An mi did deh mek some soup one evening, suh mi pick off a few peas fi put inna di pot. Miss Vera si mi pick di peas, and yuh know wah she do, Greg?"

Curious now, Greg asked, "Wah Granny do?"

"Miss Vera dash hot wata 'pon di peas shoot dem an kill dem." I looked him straight in the face. "Because she see seh mi did ah use dem. Jus like dat, she kill off di whole a di peas dem. All because she see dem coulda help mi."

35

CHASTISED

VERA

I would have preferred if Greg had listened to me and left Junior alone, but he was a grown man now—even if he was Flo's wash belly. He came back into the house and said nothing of his conversation with Morris's son. I was terrified that once Greg left, Junior would come to my wing of the house and start an argument, for I'd seen it in his eyes—he wanted no peace.

Greg and I talked until Morris came home, and after he got settled, Greg called the two of us together and did a terrible thing. The moment he opened his mouth and his brows met in the middle, I knew I couldn't stop him—not once the boy had made up his mind. I knew I had no hope.

My youngest grandson stood there and told me—me, his granny—that I should make peace with Junior. He also said he didn't want to hear any more complaining about Morris. Said I should just live in peace with my husband.

"Granny, you're a grown woman—over eighty years old," he said, like a reprimand. "Stop complaining about Mass Morris."

I suddenly pulled back and cried out, "Greg! Jesus!" But he wouldn't stop. Morris stood there beside him, just as shocked.

"Granny," Greg said, "you're an older woman now. You should be a peaceful woman. Sit down and read your Bible or something. Stop creating division between father and son."

I began to weep. I hadn't expected Greg to do what he did. I knew he meant well—but he didn't understand what I was going through. It felt like no one in Canada understood, and I'd been begging Mammy and Daddy to take me back. I had been trying so hard.

But Greg had come all this way only to admonish me, right there in front of Morris. And I could hardly defend myself.

After he left, I said nothing to Morris. There was nothing to say. Greg had already told us both that he expected peace—and no more quarrels.

Vera

FLO'S VISITS TO JAMAICA HAD BECOME MORE FREQUENT, FOR SHE AND Auntie Pet had met a pastor from Jamaica during his visit to Canada. The pastor's church was located in Bethel Town, Discovery Bay—a little church set high upon a hill.

On the last day of the convention, I made the journey with Pastor Guthrie's church to Bethel Town. The drive was long, but when we arrived, the church was packed with visitors from congregations all across the island. The day was hot, but the breeze was refreshing, and like the old days, the sound of the drums and the many voices singing together filled my heart with joy. It took me, an old woman, some time to get up the steep hill—but I made it, though out of breath. And Greg, my grandson, was pleased to see me.

But during the service, I found I couldn't get comfortable. I kept fidgeting, distracted. My head began to spin, and I suddenly felt the urge to run from the church. I began to weep, unable to stop the sudden wave of fear that struck me—right there in God's house.

I exited so quickly that it caused a scene, but I couldn't help myself.

Flo didn't see me leave, but someone must have sent for her. My daughter did all she could to keep her voice low, for there were many bystanders watching outside the church. Then Greg arrived and calmed her, for she had been so worried. My sudden exit, my unexplainable weeping—it had all seemed strange.

Greg assured his mother he would handle the situation. After Flo reluctantly returned inside, he led me to a massive tree, where we both sat on a large boulder in the shade. He wrapped his arm around me.

"Granny, what's wrong?"

I couldn't explain it. I was weeping. "Greg, mi fraid."

"Afraid of what, Granny?" He caressed my shoulder. "Why yuh afraid? You're at church."

I shrugged. "Mi...mi..." I saw people watching us, but Greg didn't seem to care. He was gentle, patient, coaxing the answer from me.

"Di singing dem...dem ah watch mi."

Greg looked around, puzzled. "What things, Granny? What's watching you?"

I pointed up toward the sky. And seeing them, I became even more afraid. I wept again. Greg followed my gaze, and his face grew solemn. A flock of vultures—jancros, as we call them—circled high above the church.

"Si dem...dem deh watch mi!"

"Granny, it's okay, they're just flying...that's all."

But I didn't believe him. I remembered too well: a jancro had been sent to harm Flo many years before.

Still, I felt suddenly calmed by Greg's embrace. His arms around me were like a shield.

"Nuh worry, Granny," he said softly. "Cum, let's go back into the church..."

Vera

With every telephone call, I begged Keith and Flo to bring me back to Canada, for I could no longer endure the struggle with Morris. Money was going missing from the house—someone was coming in and stealing it from me. Morris would always say he had no idea where my money had gone. I spoke with Keith about it.

"Daddy, mi cyan tek ih."

I wanted them to send for me, but Flo said they had already tried. My attempts to get another visa were futile; Canadian immigration said I was too old. How could they say that to me? They shouldn't have, for with every look in the mirror, I still saw the same face I had seen all my life. I was over eighty years old, yet I hardly had wrinkles. It was the aches and pains that slowed me down.

After months of pleading, I finally got my answer. Flo and Greg returned to Jamaica because I had agreed to leave Morris. I wouldn't be going to Canada but would instead move to the Amy Mushette Home For The Aged. I had been confirmed at Saint Michael's Anglican Church for some time; Morris and I had been members there, and while I still loved to sing, it was Morris who joined the choir. I preferred to sing alone.

The Amy Mushette Home For The Aged was located in Duncans, operated by the Anglican Diocese of Jamaica. Flo and Greg had met with Father—a good man—and it was decided I would be accepted there. The following day, after Morris left, Flo and my grandson came for me with a driver. As quickly as we could, we gathered my things—

only the essentials, for Morris had not been told I was leaving. I wanted it that way.

I told Greg that day how all my money had been stolen from the house. But I became confused and embarrassed when Greg found the money.

"Granny," Greg said, exchanging a quick glance with his mother, "si di money here."

"Mama!" Flo shook her head as she took the money from Greg's hand. "Nobody nuh tek yuh money." She counted it out so I could see, then pointed toward my suitcase—where Greg had found it, wrapped up and stuffed away. He had found it, just like he always had since he was a boy—always finding things.

"Mama, yuh money deya all along."

I sat at the edge of the bed, shaking my head, unable to explain. I had no recollection of stashing the money away. I sat there in silence as my things were packed, wondering what had happened to me. Deep inside, I was enveloped in sorrow, ashamed and confused.

Later, just before we left, I sat on the veranda with Greg and Flo. The driver stood just on the steps. I didn't know the man, but he told me he was from Bethel Town, where Pastor Benbow's church was. Pastor Stanley Benbow had been that young boy of thirteen who stood with me by the riverside the day we were baptized. Years had passed, and now, as an old woman, I was to be his ward. Pastor would have the task of visiting me, taking me to the doctor, and doing all the things Keith and Flo couldn't do, for they were away in Canada.

Greg stood on the veranda, clearly impatient and ready to go. His hands dug deep into his pockets as he watched me carefully tie a scarf around my head. But as I sat there, my thoughts were with Morris. I loved him and could hardly bear the thought of leaving him, but I needed to go. I couldn't face him and say goodbye, so I thought it best to leave without a word.

"Granny, are you sure about this...about leaving?" Greg asked. He looked to his mother. "Mommy, maybe we should wait and talk to Mass Morris. Then we can go. She should at least tell him. Im a-go come back to di empty house..."

I quickly interrupted and explained why I felt I should leave. I was nearly done tying the scarf, one end cascading over my shoulder. "When I was young," I said, "I was a pretty woman... and I could have any man I wanted. Mi pick Morris... I chose him. After all I did for him, he shouldn't treat mi like dis."

I saw Flo nod in agreement as she turned to Greg. "It's true. She worked and took care of him—even when he went to prison."

"Morris nuh have no right fi treat me suh..."

With Greg's urging, and his help to get me ready, we gathered my things. I told Flo and Greg to go through my buffet. "Tek anything unuh want."

Flo gasped at the sight of an old tankard. My child's eyes widened at the sight of it. The tankard was made of clay, stained a glossy beige, and printed with the words *Tennent's Stout*.

Flo took the little clay jug and said, "Ma Jane jug!" She hugged the tankard to her chest. "Shi used to put goat's milk in deh!" I smiled at my daughter, not expecting her to remember it. Ma Jane had used that large clay jug to keep goat's milk, even when I was a child. I nodded with pleasure when Flo passed her hand over it. After she explained it to Greg, he grabbed the jug. For a moment, mother and son struggled to claim it. Flo didn't give up, and Greg eventually let go. But I saw in his eyes that he had resolved that one day it would be his.

I left the house holding back tears, not knowing when I would see it again. I didn't say goodbye to Junior. We made one stop before the driver took us away from Hyde. I stopped to say goodbye to one of my closest friends and left her my cherished set of cutlery—a set I had brought back from Canada. Then I was gone.

My heart ached, for I hadn't seen Morris to tell him goodbye, but I thought of the last time I saw him—early that morning as he pushed his bicycle through the gate, oblivious to the fact that he would return to a house without a wife. We stopped briefly in Clark's Town, where I said goodbye to Astley Brown—Mass Astley, as everyone called him. Astley and Flo had been friends for many years, and when they were young, he, Flo, and Pet had been close members of Bredda Nattie's church in Bottom Town.

Astley had lost his hearing many years ago, but it hadn't stopped him from becoming a successful businessman. His grocery shop must have been the first in Bottom Town. I thought of everything and everyone I was leaving behind, and I wanted to scream aloud—tell Flo I'd changed my mind. But we were already well on our way from Clark's Town, and there was no turning back.

36

AMY MUSHETTE HOME FOR
THE AGED

Amy Mushette Home for the Aged sat on a wide stretch of land, not far from the main road in Duncans. Built directly across from a cemetery, it was a rather peculiar place for the elderly to spend the winter of their lives. But that was the least of Vera's concerns. She'd been settled in her own room, quite content with her new living arrangements.

The woman running the place had seemed nice at first—at least, that's what Vera had thought. But over the last several weeks, she had shown herself to be the most cunning of women. In charge of the home, she smiled and agreed with every word Flora said during her visits. But the moment Flora left, she became a different person—hardly paying attention to any of the elderly folk the way she did when their families were around.

Pastor Benbow visited often enough, usually on Saturdays, and he always brought the nicest of treats for Vera. He'd even left a large container for her to store them in. She enjoyed the pastor's counsel, and if he couldn't visit, his wife would. But more than anything, Vera wanted to see Morris again. She missed him so.

One morning, she woke determined that she would go home. She got up early with a plan, and just before lunch—when the sun was hot

—Vera made certain she was not seen. She set out for the main road, telling herself she would walk to Clark's Town if she had to. Morris needed her. She should never have left him.

Over and over during the long nights, Vera had worried. *Wah Morris a-go eat tonight?* The thought wouldn't leave her. She had begged those in charge to let her go home. The answer had always been "No."

By the time Vera reached the road, she was exhausted. She paused, thinking back to the days when she walked to the market, or long before adulthood, when she played with her sisters all day beneath the blazing sun. Back then, she'd been invincible. She worked two, sometimes three jobs in a week—even in a single day—and still came home with energy to cook and clean.

But now, walking toward the main road, she could feel her strength failing. Her back ached. Her heart pounded. She realized, suddenly, that she hadn't even dressed properly for the long journey she'd planned so late the night before. No money. No bag. Not even her good shoes.

Vera paused to look down. She was still wearing her house slippers.

And that's when she heard them—the two helpers from Amy Mushette Home. With her back bent, Vera tried to hurry, to get away. But she could hardly move. A vision of her young self gave her strength.

"Dem cyan ketch mi," she said softly, urging herself to run with all her might.

Then again, "Lela couldn't ketch mi…"

But it wasn't Lela chasing her that afternoon beneath the burning sun.

And just like those days—when she'd finally grown tired after a long run from Lela—Vera's energy gave out. She fell forward on the dirt road.

The two brutes got to her. All Vera could do was lie there in protest. She screamed Morris's name over and over.

"Morris! Mek mi guh ah mi yawd!"

They restrained her, even as she clawed at their eyes—just like she'd done to Lela when they were little girls. The two women dragged her along the dirt road, and Vera got cuts all over her knees.

THE WEEKS AT THE AMY MUSHETTE HOME TURNED INTO MONTHS, AND with every passing day, Vera longed to return home. Pastor made extra visits in his efforts to resolve the ongoing conflict between Vera and the woman in charge, for Vera was convinced she was a wicked woman. She had stopped eating the food they prepared, and with every call from Canada, she told Flora how much she wanted to leave. The staff, she claimed, had been taking things—even stealing from the snack box the pastor had so kindly stocked for her.

One early morning, Vera made her way down the long corridor to the main office. Just outside the door, she paused. From there, she overheard them talking—them, the wicked woman and her staff. They were conspiring, speaking plainly about putting pills in her food.

She'd been right all along.

From that day, Vera refused anything unless she saw it prepared herself, or it came from one of the few staff she liked and trusted. She saw the others for who they were. Heard them with her own ears. So she took nothing.

God bless Pastor, Vera thought. *If not fi di snacks him bring, mi woulda dead long time.*

She had thought of home so many times. But after weeks of longing, she gave up hope of ever seeing her Morris again. Then, one day—when she least expected it—Morris showed up.

Vera was sitting in the main hall when she saw him. They spoke quietly, and Vera asked only for his forgiveness—for leaving him behind. But Morris seemed well. He'd even brought some of her favourite things to eat: fruits, bread, and mangoes.

"Morris," she said, her voice trembling, "yuh aright?"

"V, of course mi aright."

She could no longer hold back her sorrow.

"Morris... mi waan cum home..."

He smiled. The partially toothless grin she knew so well was gone —he had new dentures now.

"V," he said gently, as he always had, "Mi neva tell yuh fi leave..."

And just like that, the conversation was over.

Morris had given his answer.

He didn't want her back.

Vera wept. She remembered what he had always told her. What he had promised.

He said he would never leave her.

But she had left him without saying goodbye.

———————

———————

———————

THE SITUATION AT THE AMY MUSHETTE HOME FOR THE AGED worsened over time. In the opinion of Saint Michael's Anglican Church, as well as the staff and the woman who ran the home, Vera Belford was a cantankerous old woman who brought more trouble than the monthly payments from her family in Canada were worth.

But to her daughter and grandchildren back in Canada, Vera was the same Granny they had always known and loved. They still heard the same voice, the same uncontrollable laughter that brought tears to her eyes when she found something truly funny. To them, Granny spoke of the past as though she'd just left it moments ago. She was still the woman who praised God for journeying mercies when they arrived from abroad, who placed her hands upon their heads and prayed through tears, asking God to guide their every step. She was the same granny who sat up late in her little kitchen making coconut drops just for them.

Flora had visited Jamaica several times and had taken her mother to the doctor. A diagnosis of early-stage dementia had come as a shock. For several weeks, the medications worked, and the reports on Flora's mother were encouraging—until Vera discovered what the new pills were for. After that, Flora learned that her mother had been hiding the pills wherever she could—inside pillows, beneath her mattress, even outside the window.

During a surprise visit, Flora kept herself hidden, hoping to see what her mother was really experiencing. The woman she observed that morning could not have been her mother. When Flora finally spoke to her, Vera sat still and listened, her only protest being that the staff had stolen several items of her clothing.

On her next visit, Flora brought her son Garth. This time, they discovered something else troubling. Due to a severe outbreak of seborrheic dermatitis, Garth made the decision to shave his grandmother's head—the infection had spread to her face.

"Whaap'm, Wy-wa!" he said with a grin. Granny smiled right back. Garth had always made her laugh. He knew how to distract her from anything that troubled her.

With his mother standing nearby, Garth gently broke the news.

"Granny, guess what?"

She looked up, smiling. "Mi waan give yuh a new hairstyle." Garth said.

Vera chuckled, but the moment she noticed the scissors and shears in his hands, her smile vanished.

"Garth, no! Mi cyan cut off mi hair," she said, her brows drawn tight with fear and resolve.

"Mama, yuh nuh have no choice," Flora said, holding up a mirror. "Look deh... it soon cover yuh face, Mama."

Vera began to weep. The memory of her childhood rushed in like a flood—being sick, stuck in bed while her sisters played outside in the sun. Losing her hair. Ma Jane's stern emerald eyes watching over her.

"Mammy, mi cyan cut off mi hair, Mammy..." she whispered, lost in the memory.

Despite her protests, Vera eventually conceded. Garth trimmed her hair while she wept. But by the time he was done, he had her laughing again.

"Ih soon grow back, Granny. Nuh worry," he said.

VERA WAS EIGHTY-EIGHT WHEN GREG PAID A SURPRISE VISIT THE following year. She was sitting in the main hall with the other residents when she saw the tall figure enter. Her eyesight had weakened, and all she could see was the silhouette against the bright light at the door. The figure came closer and sat next to her, grinning.

"Greg?"

"Yes, Granny..." He took her hands, kissed her face.

"Lawd, Jesus! Greg?" Vera wept and smiled at once. "Yuh cum look fi Granny?"

In her room, she told Greg everything. She wasn't happy at the home. Greg tried to explain why finding another place was difficult. The Amy Mushette Home was close to Pastor Benbow, who visited often. If anything went wrong, he could get there quickly. But she hardly seemed to understand.

When the woman in charge of the home was dismissed and news came that one of Vera's oldest friends had taken over, the family in Canada was relieved. At first. Within weeks, that friendship had dissolved. Vera was convinced this woman—who was close in age to her own daughter—was also wicked and determined to make her life miserable.

Things escalated quickly.

Greg returned to Jamaica to try and resolve the conflict. But his granny was headstrong, resolute in her feelings. The new matron spoke of terrible things Miss Vera had said, and repeated remarks Vera had made about her to the staff. Greg stood in the main kitchen, stunned by what he heard.

The day before he flew back to Canada, Greg was handed a letter to deliver to his mother. After reading it, he phoned his parents immediately.

Vera Belford had been discharged from the Amy Mushette Home for the Aged, effective the first of the following month.

IT TOOK SEVERAL DAYS OF HARD WORK TO FIND A NEW HOME FOR VERA, and she tried to do as much as she could to get herself organized, though Pastor Benbow had assured her that his wife and several church sisters would help pack and move her. Vera was to be relocated to Brookhaven Home for the Elderly, situated between Falmouth and Duncans. She could hardly wait for the day to come when she would finally leave the place that had brought her so much misery.

Pastor Benbow visited often, though he explained he wouldn't be able to be there on the day she moved.

"Alright, Sister Vera," he'd said gently, "Nuh worry yuhself."

Vera began to cry again. "Pasta," she said, not bothering to wipe away the tears, "Dem wicked! Dem tek weh all mi sumting dem... Dem teif weh all mi tings..."

He took her hand in his.

"Sister Vera, yuh cyan worry yuhself," he said, and prayed with her until she was calm.

Before leaving, he promised everything would be fine. "Sister Dimple wi come inna di mawning an sekkle off everyting." Vera looked into his dark, kindly face and saw the same little boy who had taken his watery baptism with her that Sunday so long ago. She couldn't remember exactly how old she'd been that day—but she remembered him, those eyes. She began to weep once more. Only God, she thought, could have sent this good man back into her life after so many years.

"Pasta, God bless yuh," she whispered, squeezing his hand.

The next morning, Vera refused the breakfast brought to her, choosing instead to break her fast with something from the small box of snacks she kept hidden in her room. She no longer trusted the staff. She'd done her best to tidy herself, proud even at nearly ninety years old.

Her youngest grandson, Greg, had been the last to visit her at the Mushette Home. Now she was to leave for Brookhaven. It was time to start again.

Pastor's wife, Sister Dimple, arrived with two other women. Together, they packed Vera's belongings with care. When everything was ready and they began to help her out of the room, Vera—though stricken with back pain—tried her best to walk upright, supported on either side.

"Tek yuh time, Miss Vera," one of the sisters said gently.

"Yes, love," encouraged the other, "tek yuh—"

Suddenly, a loud bang echoed through the hallway.

Vera jumped. The three women froze, startled. Their eyes blazed with fury.

From the kitchen, several of the Mushette staff emerged, each holding old pots and pans. As Vera walked toward the front door, they began to bang the cookware with large wooden spoons, their laughter rising like smoke. They jeered, calling her names, mocking her departure.

Vera kept quiet. Her spine was fragile, but her pride stood straight. She lifted her chin, refused to let them see her cry. She walked on with dignity, flanked by the women who came to help her.

Even as she was helped into the vehicle, the staff continued their crude send-off, banging pots as if to mock her existence. But Vera never turned around.

The car pulled away from the Amy Mushette Home for the Aged.

And Vera never looked back.

37

FLORA

F lora walked into Brookhaven Home and found her mother seated out on the second-floor terrace. She'd been visiting every day since arriving in Jamaica, and it hadn't been easy.

She had tried everything to help her mother find peace with the young woman in charge at Brookhaven, but it was no use.

All this time, Flora had thought Vera was just being difficult... but now, looking back, it was impossible to say when her mother's dementia had truly begun. For all she knew, her mother had been unwell long before she was moved from her home in Hyde.

Flora watched her and smiled sadly. This was the woman she'd always known to be so strong and proud—never willing to give another the last word. But as the memories drifted through her, things started to make sense. The issues between her mother and Mr. Morris would have only grown worse had she not moved her when she did.

Mr. Morris, too, was suffering. His illness had taken hold more severely. He had forgotten nearly everything—even his own wife. Now under the care of his son, Mr. Morris spent his days indoors under a watchful eye. He would wander through the house and roam the old roads for hours, living entirely in the past.

Whenever Flora visited, he spoke only of long ago.

"Yes, man... yes, Flo," he'd say, eyes lost in the sunset. "Ah suh it guh... bwoy, it nuh easy. Mi jus come from out deh, yuh know... jus come from grung..."

Junior was always nearby, rubbing his father's shoulders before guiding him gently back to his chair.

"Miss Flo," he said once, shaking his head, "Ah suh him gwaan all di time... him jus live inna di past."

But now Flora let go of the memories of her stepfather and focused on her mother, who sat gazing at the vehicles passing on the road below.

"Mammy... how Daddy?"

"Keith aright, Mama."

"How Bill? An' Courtney?"

"Everybody aright, Mama."

Flora took a deep breath. What she had to say next wouldn't go over well.

"Mama, mi cyan move yuh again... suh yuh muss behave yuhself, Mama..."

Her mother didn't answer, just stared at the road, her brow drawn together.

Flora knew exactly what she was thinking—that her own daughter didn't believe a word she'd said about the "wicked woman" who ran Brookhaven. Flora understood her mother was unwell, but moving her again simply wasn't possible. She'd already discussed it with Keith, and they'd agreed that no matter where she was moved, the issues would likely follow.

Her mother didn't speak. Her jaw was set, chin held high, just like always when she was displeased. But it was the silence that said everything—Flora knew too well that her mother rarely kept quiet when she was content.

"Mama, yuh know yuh birthday soon come?" she asked gently, trying to lift the mood. "Yuh know how old yuh going to be?"

Her mother looked at her with a puzzled expression, as if trying to do the math in her head.

"Mama," Flora smiled, "yuh birthday is on Christmas Day. How old will you be?"

Vera Wallace looked up at her and said, without hesitation:

"Thirty."

Flora couldn't smile. She knew, in that moment, her mother truly believed it.

"No, Mama... yuh going to be ninety."

A look of shock swept over her mother's face, and then she began to weep. She had always been a vain woman. Even now, the thought of old age was unbearable to her.

Before leaving Jamaica, Flora sat down for a long talk with her mother. She had to tell her the truth.

"Mama," she said louder than usual, her mother's hearing not what it used to be, "I'm going to have surgery... heart surgery."

Her mother wept again. But Flora knew she had to tell her. She needed her to understand.

38

COME AWAY

Vera's youngest grandchild, Greg, visited her in 2013 at Brookhaven Home for the Aged—and she recognized him instantly.

Her grandson stood smiling, surprised that she still knew him, even at the age of ninety.

"Lawd Jesus," she said aloud, eyes filling with tears. "Greg? Oh God... Greg, yuh come look fi Granny... God bless yuh."

"Yes, Granny..."

To him, she still looked the same—but she'd lost so much weight, and seemed so tiny now. Not the strong granny he'd always known.

"How Mammy?" she asked, looking Greg square in the eye. "I know she cyan come," she said, her voice low. "But every day I lift my hands up to Jesus... and I pray."

She paused, shaking her head. "Oh God... mi one dawta."

"Granny... she's good. The surgery went okay."

"Jesus." Vera cringed, shaking her head in sympathy.

"But," Greg continued, "she cyan travel..."

His granny leaned closer.

"Greg, Granny cyan hear suh good again—wah yuh seh?"

He moved close to her ear. "Mommy... she can't travel yet. To come see you."

She nodded slowly. "I know, I understand. Poor Flo... mi one dawta..."

"So, Granny—how yuh doing?"

"Lawd Jesus. Pain! Di back."

Then she looked around quickly, just to make sure none of the staff were nearby. Lowering her voice, she said, "Di gal deh... di one dem call nurse. Wicked!" She took a deep breath.

"Granny, don't worry about that stuff," Greg replied with a smile. "Let's change the subject. Did you find a new boyfriend yet? I see a few single men downstairs—and there's one man with no legs... what about him?"

Her brows converged in mock disapproval, but she burst out laughing and fanned him away with her hand.

"Greg!" she exclaimed, but the laughter lingered in her eyes.

Then she surprised him.

"Yuh go look fi Morris?"

"Yes, Granny."

"How him is?"

"Good."

He couldn't bring himself to say that the love of her life barely remembered her anymore.

"Wen yuh go back, tell Morris him must behave himself... an him must listen to Junior."

"Okay, Granny."

"Oh God... Morris." She drifted, eyes unfocused.

Greg gently touched her arm. "What yuh thinking?"

She shook her head, smiling. "Mi cyan tell yuh..."

He was sure her thoughts were of her husband—but he didn't press.

After a long silence, she finally said, almost in a whisper,

"Morris come an knock the door every night when mi go sleep... always deh ask fi mi open di door."

Greg didn't say a word.

He just held her hand—and listened to his granny's thoughts.

———

———

———

FLORA RECEIVED HER DOCTOR'S PERMISSION TO TRAVEL IN AUGUST OF 2013—but at her own risk. Still, she was adamant: it was time to visit her mother. They hadn't seen each other since 2011.

Her youngest son had pleaded with her to wait a little longer. But she refused.

"You may go," Greg said, "but I go with you."

The following month, Greg and his parents traveled to Jamaica to visit his granny.

The day they arrived at Brookhaven, Greg ascended the stairs quickly and found his grandmother seated on the couch in the main lounge, surrounded by other elderly residents.

It took her several moments to recognize him—then she began to weep.

She was smaller now. Weaker.

He hugged her close, pressing his face against hers as she cried, for he sensed this might be their last meeting.

His granny turned to an old woman seated beside her, and though her speech was slurred, her words were clear enough.

"Is my grandson," she said. "...Is the last one... my last grandson."

Greg heard his mother's slow, laboured steps on the stairs behind him. Within moments, mother and daughter would be reunited.

His father appeared first, smiling—and somehow, his granny recognized him at once. Her eyes widened with joy.

Greg turned. His mother was making her way up the stairs, her cane in one hand, the other held by his father. She wore a dress of black and red.

And when his granny saw her—her only daughter—her body trembled.

Flo was only steps away when her mother raised both arms, mouth wide in wordless awe, silent joy.

Then the embrace.

His mother held her, and Vera—his granny—exhaled deeply before letting out a long, uncontrollable sob.

Greg quietly stepped out onto the terrace.

Later, Keith sat beside his mother-in-law and gently pinched her cheek. She smiled, her grin toothless.

Her hair had turned the softest shade of silver, though her eyebrows remained black as coal.

She spoke slowly, gently—it seemed to take all her energy just to smile.

"Granny," Keith said, "which song yuh a-go sing fi Daddy?"

She looked away, thoughtful. "*Christ Have Mercy*," she slurred.

Then she began to sing.

Her skinny feet tapped the ground like a metronome.

For a brief moment, it seemed she'd gone somewhere else—somewhere far from that room, far from them.

She was Vera Wallace again.

Perhaps she was on a stage somewhere deep in a labyrinth of memory. She tilted her head and smiled as she sang.

And when Keith rubbed her shoulder gently, she stopped.

"Aright, Granny... yuh still sing good... aright... done now."

She clasped both hands upon her lap.

———

———

———

SHE WOKE EARLY ONE MORNING KNOWING EXACTLY WHAT SHE HAD TO DO.

Flora lay awake for a while before speaking. "Keith."

"Yes, Mackie," he replied. That was what he'd always called her.

"I have to see Mama. Mi need fi guh back ah Jamaica."

It was December. They had already visited her mother in September of that same year, but Flora felt it in her spirit—she had to go again.

Keith didn't ask why. He only said, "Okay."

They left the following week, planning to spend Christmas with her mother.

Vera Wallace turned ninety-one on December 25th.

They visited her daily. Vera spoke very little now—it seemed to take so much out of her just to form the words. Still, it was clear she recognized them. Some days, the woman who had once been so strong and full of fire would only lie in silence, eyes open, breathing softly.

Flora and Keith stayed in Jamaica for three months.

By March of 2014, Vera had grown weaker with each passing day. She ate almost nothing—only sips of water now and then.

On Sunday, March 2nd, Flora decided to stay home while Keith made the trip to Falmouth alone.

At first, she barely seemed to recognize him. But then, from time to time, she would look up and say quietly:

"Daddy?"

Keith nodded. "Yes, Granny. Ah Daddy."

She touched his face.

He sat with her in silence for a while. Then, gently, he lifted the glass.

"Cum, Granny...drink fi Daddy."

She drank—just a single tablespoon of water. He waited a few moments longer, holding her hand.

Then he left.

Keith had just boarded the minibus headed back to Bethel Town when the call came from Brookhaven.

Vera Belford Wallace was gone.

39

GRANNY

Vera Wallace-Belford was laid to rest on March 22, 2014, at Duncans Cemetery, just across from the Amy Muschette Home for the Aged. It had been her wish to be buried there.

The love of her life, Morris Belford, passed away the following month and was buried in Clark's Town.

At Vera's funeral, her sister, Lela Gordon, spoke of the life they had shared. Lela was ninety-four years old at the time. As she had always been, she spoke with boldness and conviction—ever the embodiment of a strong woman.

With clear eyes and unwavering voice, Lela acknowledged a solemn truth: she was now the last of the sisters left behind.

Lela Gordon—known to many as Aunt Lela—passed away three years later, at the age of ninety-seven.

JAMAICAN WORDS PRONUNCIATION

A.

a: [ah] to be, am, is
ah: it is, it's, to
afta: after
a-fe: [ah-fee] It's for
a-go, a guh: I am going, to go
an: and
anno: it's not/it wasn't
anuh: it's not/it wasn't
aright: alright
awah: what, what is it?

B.

backa: behind
baide: bath, bathe
bak chat: back talk
bawn: born
bax: slap
beenie: small
betta: better

breda/bredda: brother
blow wow: an exclamation similar to "Wow"
bwoy: boy
badda: bother
bud: bird

C.

Caca faat!: hot Damn!/holy shit, what the hell etc.
criss: ok, good, nice
cyan: [kay-an] cannot
cum: come
cuss: swear, quarrel, curse
chrismus: christmas
cyar: car
chubble: trouble
cruff: worthless Person
couldn: couldn't

D.

dash: throw
dash weh: throw away
dat: that
dawta: daughter, used by many men to refer to a woman
de: [dee] the
deh: [day] there, also use to describe a couple (mi an ar deh)
deh deh: over there, there
deh ere: is there
dehso: there, at that spot. Used to refer to a specific spot
deh bout: about, nearby, around
deya: here (me dehya = I'm around, I'm here)
dehyah: here
dem: them
dem deh: those
den: then
dis: this

di: the
dutchy: cast-iron pot with a round bottom
dutty: dirty
dweet: do it
du, duh: do
dung: down
drape up: to treat someone roughly,
holding them by their clothes

E.

eediat: idiot
everyweh: everywhere
everyting criss: everything is ok
eveling: evening or to say 'good evening'; Gud eveling Missah Right.

F.

facety: rude, feisty
farin: foreign
Fawty Leg: centipede
fadda: father
falla: follow
fraidy fraidy: easily afraid
fram: from
fe: for
fi: to
fram: from

G.

gal, gyal: girl
gimmi: give me
ginnal: con Artist
grindsman: stallion
gwaan: go on
gwey: go away
guh: go, goes

gud: good
gwaan: go on
grung: ground, also means fields food/crops grow
gwine: going to

H.

har: her
hab: have
haffi: have to
han: hand
han miggle: palm of one's hand
how yuh duh: how are you doing

I.

ital: [eye-tall] natural, organic
Im: [im] him, her
iez: ears
ih: it
inna: into, in the
im: him / her

J.

jancro: vulture that is a scavenger, John Crow
jacket: bastard child

K.

ketch: catch, find
kibba yuh mouth!: shut your mouth
Kiss mi neck!: Kiss my neck (as in 'what the heck')
kraw: scratch
kya: care, ie: mi nuh kya (I don't care)

L.

labrish: gossip
latta: later

lakka: like
lawd: lord
Lawd a massi!: lord have mercy
leff/lef: Leave/Left
leggo: let go, out of control
lickkle: little/ small
lik: hit/knock
luk: look

M.

madda: mother
man of de yaad: man of the house
mareena: wife beater tank top
mash up: to destroy, tear down, break up
mawga: meagre, skinny
mawning, mawnin: morning
mek: make, let
mekhace/mikhace: make haste, hurry up
mi: I
Missah: mister
Mass: mister
mout: mouth
mooma: mother
mum: a pet name, pronounced, moom,
murda: murder
muss: must
muma: mother
example: cum, mum (as is to say come baby, or darling etc.)
monkey face: To tease, stick out your tongue, make funny face

N.

nex: next
neva: never
nuh: not, don't
nuff: plenty

numba: number
nuttin: nothing

O.

ow: how
obeah: [obee-ah] a brand of witchcraft practiced in Jamaica
obeah man: witch Doctor
oddah: other
odda: other

P.

pasta: pastor
pickney/pickni: child, children
peenie wallie: firefly
pon: on
pum pum: vagina, female genital

R.

rassclat/raasclaat: [raws-clot] a curse word,
rolling calf: a ghost that appears as a red eyed bull that hauls heavy
chains behind it and haunts the earth at night
rock-stone mouth: an alternate phrase for cursing

S.

sey: say
sekkle: settle
shi: she
shoulda: shoulder
si: see
sista, sistah: sister
singting: something
sumting: something
sizzas: scissors
sum: some
sumady: somebody

smaddy: somebody
sugga: sugar
suh: so

T.

tan: stay
tek: take
teif: theif
tallowah: strong or fearless, Very strong-willed, fearless
ting: things
tree: three
town: short for Kingston (Jamaica's capital city)
tun: turn

U.

unuh: [oon-new] you all
uno: you all (or both of you)
unda: [on-da] under

W.

Waan: want
Wah, wa: what
wa mek: how come, why
wata: water
watchya: watch this
whaap'm: what happened
wen: when
whey, weh: where, what
wata: water
wi: will
wi: we, us, our, ours
wid: with
winda: window
worlian: Materialistic person; ungodly person
wuk: work

Y.

    Yah: here
    yaad, yawd: yard, house, home
    yuh: [yoo] you
    yuhself: yourself
    yai: eye

www.ingramcontent.com/pod-product-compliance
Lightning Source LLC
Chambersburg PA
CBHW021951090426

42811CB00041B/2407/J